Waiting to be Wanted

A Stepmom's Guide to Loving Before Being Loved

Cheryl Shumake

D1570241

Waiting to be Wanted: A Stepmom's Guide to Loving Before Being Loved
©2021 by Cheryl Shumake

Published by Stepmom Sanity and The Inspired Studio, LLC
Edited by AsharaYlana Editing Services
Cover Design by The Inspired Studio

The persons and events portrayed in this book have been used with permission. To protect the privacy of these individuals, some names and identifying details have been changed.

Library of Congress Control Number: 2020925722

ISBN: 978-1-7364025-0-4 (Paperback)
ISBN: 978-1-7364025-2-8 (Ebook)

Printed in the United States of America

Dedicated to the very special women who open both their hearts and arms to children who may never acknowledge them. God sees you, Stepmom. The jewels in your crown are BEAUTY-FULL.

Soli Deo Gloria

TABLE OF CONTENTS

Hello Dear Stepmom Sisters,

Thank you so much for adding Waiting to be Wanted to your toolkit. It is humbling to be invited into your Stepmom Journey and I want you to know I do not hold this privilege lightly.

I also want you to know this project has been bathed in prayer. Every word has been written with you in the forefront of my thoughts, and my heart lifted in prayer to the Father on your behalf. I am sure you will be blessed by the stories, help, and hope you will find between the covers. I am equally sure this work is inadequate to address every challenge you face in the journey. God has a unique calling for you, and, although this book will discuss general principles, there are specific ways in which He wants to act in your family. My pastor once told us, "The minute you have a God small enough to understand, you no longer have a God big enough to worship." I can't begin to explain everything God is doing in your life. He is too big and you are too important to Him.

There are gaps, but I know the Lord will fill the gaps for you. Rely on Him as you make your way through Waiting to be Wanted. He will meet you as you read. Something He inspired me to write will inspire something in you I did not write; spark a thought, a change of direction, a "just yours" solution to a "just yours" issue. That's the Holy Spirit nudging you to dig a little deeper. As much as you've invited me into your Stepmom Journey, you're being invited into a journey of discovery of your own. Travel well.

To your step-mothering success,

Cheryl

"Instead, we were like young children among you. Just as a nursing mother cares for her children, so we cared for you. Because we loved you so much, we were delighted to share with you not only the gospel of God but our lives as well."
1 Thessalonians 2:7-8 (NIV)

HOW TO USE THIS GUIDE

Five of the devices in our home demanded my attention. Felt like 500. Beeping, dinging, ringing, and YouTube singing crowded my mind, frustrating my ability to form a coherent thought, much less comprehensible speech.

"The thing, Honey! The thing right in there!!!"

I jabbed at the air, in the general direction of our appliance cabinet as my husband stood there with a blank look on his face. Overwhelmed by the noise, and irritated by my husband's inability to decipher my gestures, I struggled to ask a simple:
"Honey, can you hand me the can opener?"

Our instant access to too much stimuli has tipped the scales towards overload. If you're like me, you have dozens of books downloaded on your tablet yet to read, videos saved yet to watch, and websites bookmarked to which you have not returned. I try to build margin in my head by skimming the information passing before my eyes rather than absorbing it, all too often missing hidden treasure. I have to slow down, silence some of the noise, or continue living with chronic stress. As well as continue missing what should be valued.

I want to encourage you to slow down as you read this book. Wring this book dry of every bit of help and hope available. Read ready to receive, to encounter God. TAKE YOUR TIME with Waiting to be Wanted. Don't put it down when it gets dicey. Sit with the tension. Remove the distractions clamoring for your attention. Read, re-read, then read again, if necessary. Take notes. Journal. Highlight and bookmark pages. You have already made a financial investment, give yourself time to realize a return on the investment of your head and heart.

There are four sections to this guide. The first three sections, The Famished Heart, The Focused Heart, and The Fruitful Heart, discuss how our motivations, experiences, and beliefs impact our ability to love while waiting to be loved. They also provide strategies to relate in transformative ways, and help you grow in love for children you did not birth. You will find a mirror in one of the sections. There is a stepmom sister within these pages whose story will resonate with you and give voice to your indecipherable feelings. You will also find stories, examples, and scriptures which do not speak directly to you, nor your situation. Just tuck away the information which does not relate to your "now" moment. Truth is never irrelevant for long. Eventually it answers a need either in our own life or the life of someone we're privileged to help.

No matter where we are, these sections will invite us to take one step further towards being a stepmom whose consistent love becomes the catalyst through which God blesses her family.
These three sections are divided into six chapters. The first chapter of each section introduces the heart posture of the moms who are famished, focused, or fruitful; followed by four chapters discussing habits and characteristics. At the end of each chapter is a segment called "Treasure Hunt" in which you have the opportunity for reflection, prayer, unearthing truths, and application. The final chapter in each section is focused on biblical truth to help you live in the freedom Christ won for you.

The last section, Prayers for the Waiting Room, includes 12 targeted prayers to help you invite God into your waiting, and surrender to Him any issues you may face. The prayers may be used verbatim, but I strongly encourage you to memorize the scriptures associated with each prayer and use those scriptures to pray as the Holy Spirit specifically leads you.

This guide will not serve the stepmom wanting to justify a crummy approach to parenting. This guide is not for the stepmom looking for ways to manipulate her children into emotional attachment so she can feel good about herself. This is not for the stepmom who believes this guide is for other stepmoms.

This guide is for the woman who values authenticity. The one willing to say, "Father God, I feel left out and lonely sometimes. What are we going to do about it?" This is for the woman who wants to parent in a way that brings honor and glory to God despite what it may or may not bring to herself. Waiting to be Wanted is for the woman who will cooperate with the Holy Spirit to bring about the necessary changes in her thinking. This is a guide for the brave. You!

WAITING WAIL

"Good things come to those who wait." What a crock!

I despised that quote in the past. Who wants to wait around for good things to happen? When someone tried to console me with an ill-placed, "good things come to those who wait," what I heard was a disguised appeal to join the ranks of the wimpy.

Legend has it the quote comes from an older version which goes like this: "Good things come to those who wait but only those things left by those who hustle!"

Now, that is more like it! Why wait when I can just go get my own good? I can handle being in control. In the driver's seat. If I hustle my way to "good things," I can have them when I say so. The formula works. Like 2 + 2 = 4. Do more + go more + be more + run more = get more. No need to wait. Just "more" your way to good things. Right. Right?

No. Not right. At all. The quote actually derived from a pathetically passive poem which is more closely aligned with truth. Wouldn't you know it?

I'd like to introduce a poem to you, titled, "*Tout vient ß qui sait attendre.*" by Violet Fane:

> 'Ah, all things come to those who wait,'
> I say these words to make me glad,
> But something answers soft and sad,
> 'They come, but often come too late.'

No disrespect intended, but as far as I'm concerned, this poem penned by Ms. Fane can kick rocks! "I say these words to make me glad." Ha! Even Ms. Fane found the words she penned hard to swallow. She wrote them to self-soothe; make herself feel better about missed opportunities and the arrival of things she did not want.

My inner dialogue in response to this poem would sound like this: "I don't want all things. I want good things. Only good things! Especially if I have to wait. Any waiting imposed on me should pay off in enormous benefit to me."

Ms. Fane suggests our efforts yield very little. As if our efforts do not control the outcome. Doesn't Ms. Fane know we live in a world which bulldozes passivity? We take action. We make things happen. Even passive writing is frowned upon. Ha!

She ends the poem with resigned submission: "They come, but often come too late." Well, then, what's the point? If things may come too late, then how helpful can waiting be?

All sarcasm aside, when I take a deeper look, my real problem with the poem is that it exposes the self-deception I still struggle to overcome. As much as I hate to admit it, for most of my life, I believed I was in control. The truth is, life happens; without my permission and irrespective of my timetable. I don't have everything well in hand. Things do come in their own time. More accurately, things come in God's time. You and I have no choice but to wait. How we wait determines if the waiting is troubled or peace-filled.

WAITING WOES
"She has no patience," I overheard my pastor say as they lifted my car out of a ditch.

Shame warmed my face as I scooted down in the driver's seat, my daughter in the backseat, my embarrassed husband standing outside with the other men, and wondered, "How did I find myself in this type of situation again?!" We had spent a pleasant enough day horseback riding on a friend's ranch. We enjoyed a bonfire, laughs, and good times with our church family. But, as any true-blue introvert knows, after 8 hours of togetherness and being "on", I was tired and cranky. With an hour-long drive still ahead of me, and a small child to tuck in, I was ready to go. Unfortunately, the person parked in front of me in the one-way, one-car width driveway, was not.

I sat in my running car for a whopping 15 minutes before I'd had enough and decided I was going to drive on the grass to get around the car in front of me...in an area where the moon and stars provide the only light at night. Did I mention, I have an astigmatism which makes it hard to see at night and the moon enjoyed a thick layer of cloud coverage?

I swung wide to the left and promptly drove into the 2-foot ditch I did not know was waiting to swallow my car. A ditch I could have avoided had I been patient.

Is there anything more bothersome than waiting, while you're waiting? As a culture, we invest countless hours to lessen the intrusion of waiting. People have made millions of dollars inventing technology that decreases wait time. Don't want to linger on hold waiting for a customer service agent to answer your call? Simply request a return call from the service department and hang up without losing your place in the phone queue. Tired of arriving at the bus stop only to wait 30 minutes for the next bus? Download an app that will let you track public transportation and knock 20 minutes off your wait time. At this moment, in some hospital conference room with a long table, white board and 12 chairs, five people attempt to design an innovative approach to minimizing emergency room wait time.

When I am stuck in a traffic jam, my mind floods with the following thoughts: "I don't have time for this!" "Why won't this person in front of me move up?!" "Are you going to let everybody in?!" "Get off my tail! Don't you see this traffic in front of me?!" "Why is it every time I change lanes, the lane I left starts going faster?"

If you could hear my thoughts when checking out of a crowded grocery store, you might hear: "Is the cashier going to tell everybody about her child's winning soccer goal?" "Why was it only after you placed the 35th item on the belt you realized you were in the 12 items or less lane?" "If this kid bumps me one more time with that cart!" and, of course, "Why is it every time I change lanes, the lane I left starts going faster?"

Annoyed thoughts. Uncharitable thoughts. Impatient thoughts. Things can get very ugly very fast when I'm inconvenienced by a 20-minute delay.

To cope with waiting, I'll sometimes listen to the radio, flip through a Reader's Digest, or look for a person for whom I can pray. Unfortunately, as evidenced by my driving into a ditch, I didn't employ coping mechanisms enough. Trouble was brewing when my foot started tapping and my right eye started twitching. I know I'm not alone in this. Not many people know how to wait well. You're out there. Reading this paragraph. Probably rolling your eyes and telling me to get on with it.

If a momentary pause in our schedule sends us careening toward a ditch, imagine the anxiety waiting days...weeks...months...or years provokes. Waiting for a chatty cashier to complete a transaction is painless compared to waiting for the heaviness of heartache to ease, or harmony to replace turmoil in a broken relationship, or for your stepchild to respond to your love for him or her. When you are suspended between what is and what you hope for, patience is much needed but hard to find.

Traffic gridlock will clear, and sooner or later you'll make it home from the grocery store. My car was eventually rescued from the ditch. Unfortunately, there is no formula to compute when, or if, a heart will respond. There is no timetable that can accurately determine when a person will love you. Some hearts remain closed longer than we believe we can endure. Some never open. Closed hearts have a way of slapping steadfastness in the face and punching patience in the chest. I want term limits where there is an open contract. Cause is present but effect is determined by the other person's receptivity. We cannot accurately forecast closure when we're waiting on a heart to open.

THE DEATH OF WHEN

A few years ago, an Easter weekend was bookended by major surgeries for our family. One surgery was pre-scheduled for the Monday following Easter Sunday; we had time to prepare to provide six weeks of extra support to my mother. The other, an emergency appendectomy, was performed on one of our kids that Good Friday.

We arrived at the hospital in time to spend 45 minutes with our daughter before the nurse wheeled her back to surgery. Then we were ushered out of the pre-op area into the surgery lobby where we proceeded to wait. We were told the procedure would take two hours, followed by recovery, and finally admittance for an overnight stay.

Have you ever noticed how time seems to stand still when you're in a hospital waiting room? It doesn't matter how long or short the wait, an eternity passes while your loved one is under the surgeon's scalpel. Considering the circumstances, we were prepared to wait for four hours before being able to visit with our daughter.

In less than two hours she was in recovery where we were able to visit, pray, and leave her in the capable hands of the hospital staff and her mom.

Our daughter progressed well. Easter Sunday dinner was delicious. At 6:00 a.m. Monday morning, my mother, a close family friend, and I, arrived at the university hospital for my mother's procedure. We were told to settle in for a four hour wait. My plan was to stick around until noon, when my mother should be in her room, run a few errands, and come back to check on her that evening. We got a bit anxious after sitting in the waiting room for six hours without an update. At eight hours we were at the clerk's desk asking to speak with someone...anyone. Twelve hours after they'd wheeled her back for surgery, my mother was finally resting in her room for her overnight stay.

Life is put on hold in waiting. Scuttled plans and rearranged schedules become the rule for those who wait. There's nothing to do but settle into the new norm and get comfortable with being uncomfortable as you wait, because no one can tell you when it will be over. Even the experts can be wrong. Our daughter's procedure and recovery were half the time her doctor said it would be. My mother's procedure was 8 hours longer. Neither met our expectations. Yet, the waiting came to an end. In both cases, the doctor approached us in the lobby, granted access, and ushered us through the doors to meet our recovering loved one.

Waiting on the heart of your stepchild to turn towards you is a graduate level course in unmet expectations. It doesn't matter what worked in your past relationships. It may take longer for access to be granted with your stepchild. Or shorter. What unlocked the hearts of your sister's husband's cousin's best friend's stepchildren, may not work with yours.

The book which guided the woman in your bible study group may be of no use to you. Your well-meaning grandmother says, "Hold-on, honey. Patience will pay off soon." Except sometimes it doesn't. No matter what you do.

When waiting on hearts, and, when waiting on God to move in those hearts, the most impractical question we can ask is "When?" The end of waiting happens...suddenly. One moment you're waiting, the next you're not. One moment you're under water sure you're going to die as burning lungs signal your brain, "Breathe now!" The next, you've broken the surface with deep relief as you gulp air. We don't know when. We aren't told when. We're just swimming toward the light above our heads. Hoping we make it.

"When?" is a question rarely answered, if ever.

There is purpose to waiting. Therefore, the question we need the answer to is, "What?" "God, what are You trying to teach me while I wait?" "What do I need to learn about You?" "What do You want my stepchildren to know about You?" "What shall I do while I wait?" God uses waiting to refocus our attention on what matters most. In the waiting is where God transforms those who wait.

PLAYING THE WAITING GAME

Why is it such a struggle to wait well? We've been doing it for a long time. We should be experts at waiting, yet many of us cannot get comfortable with it.

Waiting is painful and inconvenient for me. I want to be done with it but cannot escape it. With waiting comes the aggravation of lack. There's a vacuum present which I crave to fill. The tease of a wanted item, a wanted change in a relationship, or personal change, annoys me with its constant presence in my thinking and perpetual absence in my life. Like a buzzing fly I want to smash. Swatting isn't a violent enough comparison.

Waiting to be wanted is complicated. It's a topsy-turvy process in which you're okay one moment and bawling the next. The concept of waiting is simple. It's merely the interval of time between what we have and what we want. Clear. Easy. Understandable. Nonetheless, waiting is messy in its application. Waiting does not come in a neat package tied up with a bow. There are stages without sequence. Mastery of one stage does not necessarily mean there will be movement to the next.

Let's take a moment to get a clear picture of what we're in for as we wait:

STAGE 1: HOPE

Excited anticipation is usually the first stage you experience when you begin waiting. There is a sense of expectancy as you make moves toward a bonded relationship with your stepson or daughter. It feels great to spend special time together, discover a shared like, or just hang out in the kitchen. You're high from the feeling that you have sown seeds for something special and you're eager to see results.

STAGE 2: FANTASIZING

Daydreaming an idealized stepfamily life usually begins when unrealized hopes linger too long for comfort. We boost faltering hope by entertaining romantic notions. The Bible tells us that hope deferred makes the heart sick, but a longing fulfilled is a tree of life (Proverbs 13:13). It is natural to want to alleviate sickness. Since the real remedy, love returned from our child, is unavailable, we take a placebo. We revel in pleasant emotions made accessible in the dream worlds our minds create. By definition fantasizing is not based on anything solid. Eventually our hearts will remember. It is then when we're in danger of despair. If we want to keep hope alive while we wait, the best thing we can do is grab hold of God's truth and don't let go.

STAGE 3: DOUBTING

There is a difference between asking questions and feeding doubts. Questioning is good. Asking questions mean you have an inquisitive mind with a thirst for knowledge. A questioning person is good at analyzing a situation from various angles, opening understanding, identifying problems, and devising possible solutions. Doubting is different. The questioning mind seeks answers. The doubting mind sees obstacles, and becomes discouraged. Doubting begins when our heart becomes more focused on wanted changes we have not experienced, rather than on the God who is able to change our perspectives and situations.

STAGE 4: RATIONALIZATION

You'll know you've started rationalizing when you begin to justify less than loving behavior. Rationalizers use reasons that seem logical and plausible on the surface, for behaviors that are unacceptable. Even if those reasons are not true. Rationalizations are usually completely unrelated to the real motivations, but they are good enough for us to assuage guilt or shame. For example, voicing, "I didn't ask my stepdaughter to go shopping with me because she would rather be in her room" when what you meant was, "I didn't ask my stepdaughter to go shopping with me because I didn't want to risk another rebuff." The dismantling of rationalizations begins with brutal honesty with oneself.

STAGE 5: FRUSTRATION

Frustration arrives on the scene when we are annoyed or upset by our inability to progress or change a situation. Frustration and I renew our acquaintance in moments when I feel painfully powerless. If there is any situation ripe for helplessness and misunderstanding, it's living in stepfamilies. While we wait, questions that feed frustrations will pop up every now and again: "Why is this happening again?" "Why can't you just _____?" "How could you _____?" Frustration hits critical mass when those unanswerable questions play on repeat in my head.

STAGE 6: RESENTMENT

If we don't learn how to wait well, frustration will eventually lead to resentment. Resentment kills relationship potential like nothing else. Resentment cancels out affection; no show of contrition from the offending person is good enough to soothe the hurt feelings of the offended person. Resentment shows up in the waiting process when we mind-loop reasons we deserve the acknowledgement, applause, or appreciation we are not getting. When you begin describing yourself, if only in your own mind, as the put-upon victim of ungrateful stepchildren, resentment is the diet you're on.

STAGE 7: ANGER

This stage is pretty self-explanatory. It's a natural progression from resentment. Unresolved resentment leads to animosity. If you find yourself openly antagonistic, or even passively peevish, as you wait, check your heart for anger.

STAGE 8: SELF-PITY

Self-pity shows its disagreeable face when there's immoderate mourning of unfulfilled hopes. A woman indulging in self-pity displays grief over her bruised ego, or mangled heart, rather than the loss of a potentially great relationship. A "woe is me" sorrow over her own heartache dominates the thoughts of a self-pitying stepmom, to the exclusion of anyone else's need.

STAGE 9: ACCEPTANCE

This is the stage of waiting where peace begins to settle in. Acceptance acknowledges the status quo but maintains belief in God's miracle working power. Acceptance bubbles up in your heart when you make consistent, God-honoring choices in the face of "even if," i.e. "My stepchildren may never love or like me, but I'm going to love them because it pleases God."

STAGE 10: RELIEF

This stage of waiting affirms peace with the reassurance that no matter what "it" is, it's okay. This stage is beyond acceptance. This is the stage where you completely let go of your desires and simply enjoy being a loving stepmom. Where other stages were buttressed with anxiety, pressure and desire to see results, relief is marked by comfort, composure, and peace.

Don't be surprised when you find yourself ping-ponging between stages as you're waiting. Transformation does not happen in a straight line. Hope doesn't necessarily morph into relief. What you doubt at 10:00 a.m., you will accept at 11:00 a.m., and fantasize about at 1:00 p.m. You will take an indirect route.
It's normal to deviate. I'd be very surprised if you didn't backtrack from time to time.

Understanding the process helps us manage waiting with humor, hope, and a heart fixed on the faithfulness of God. Loving while you wait to be loved requires a refocused heart and surrendered desires. But, you're up for the challenge. I know you are because you're reading this book. You're asking God to help. You're growing. Changing. Being transformed by the grace and power of the Holy Spirit as you implement biblical principles into your waiting and loving. Be encouraged. God will faithfully complete the work He has begun in you and your family.

SECTION I

The Famished Heart

Lord, save me from myself!

MALNOURISHED MOMS

The way I responded to her you would have thought my mother asked me to repair a brain aneurysm. I sat sobbing on the couch in my family room.

"I can't do everything. I just cannot do everything!"

I was smack-dab in the middle of an emotional breakdown. Worn out from the demands of single-motherhood. Trying to be everything to everyone around me while holding down a full-time job, and going back to school, and coaching track at my daughter's middle school, and teaching, singing, trustee boarding or whatever else my hands could do at church, and being the administrator for my friend's travelling worship team, and dealing with the craziness which is the aftermath of divorce. And, and, and!

My mother's simple request sent me careening towards a nervous collapse at full tilt.

"Can you change the light bulb?"

That was it.

That question released a 15-minute cathartic bawl. By the time I dried my tears, I had determined to change. In all my doing, I forgot to keep first things first. I fed others, perhaps with the hope that doing so would fill up some areas of my life, but starved myself. I was beyond drained. I was malnourished. A malnourished, empty, mom who kept going because I was doing what I needed to do.

I was a hungry mosquito sucking its own blood; depleting rather than thriving. I would shrivel away if things didn't change. What a tragedy it would have been to get to the end of my life not having lived it.

Do you remember what it felt like to be a kid? Before the world told you where you fit in and what you were barred from trying? Before you discovered wonder and adventure were a long way's off from just around the river bend? When there was no jockeying for position, or attention? No scorekeeping, just togetherness. Back when you were free and you didn't realize you would have to change to keep from being hurt?

We lose so much when we allow the world to dictate how we "adult." Simplicity, humility and openness to instruction are lost. Generosity of emotions and keeping short accounts are tossed aside for self-protective walls barring access to our hearts. Trust and dependence are traded for self-sufficiency. By the time you're an adult, painful interactions, responsibilities, and the weightiness of "just life," snuffs out the remaining embers of childlikeness. Perhaps that's why the type of relationship Jesus invites us to enjoy with the Father seems implausible.

JESUS LOVES THE LITTLE CHILDREN

Jesus bids us to come to Him and receive freedom in exchange for bondage. Life for death. Peace for burdens. It's a no-brainer, right? Who wouldn't trade in a dime for a billion? If it were only that easy.

Jesus is quite candid. He wants us to know that the exchange, though freely offered, is costly. It will exact pride. Unrighteousness. Self-dependence. It will require us to abdicate the right to rule our lives. We must trade our desire to self-govern for His capable lordship. The exchange will also require us to recall something we lost on the way to becoming an adult. He tells us in Matthew 18:3:

And he said: "Truly I tell you, unless you change and become like little children, you will never enter the kingdom of heaven." (NIV)

When Jesus starts a sentence with, "Truly," it behooves us to pay close attention to what comes next. It has life-altering importance.

He collars a listener, and arrests their regard until awareness of everything else fades to the background.

The disciples wanted Jesus to clarify a point of contention: "Who is great in the Kingdom of heaven?" (18:1) They were adults, with adult questions. Some of them were businessmen. Like good financial stewards, they needed to know the return on their investment. "What's in it for me, Jesus?"

I can picture Jesus sitting in the shade under a tree. A dozen or so children are laughing and running around the tree as He talks to the disciples. A little boy, snacking on fruit, sits nearby, unobtrusively hanging onto every word pouring from the mouths of the adults, as children are prone to do. Suddenly Jesus beckons to the girl. Without hesitation, he stands to his feet, brushes off her tunic and walks over to Jesus. He wraps her in His outstretched arm, and places her on one bouncing leg. He looks at the disciples, indicates the trusting girl at rest on His knee and says:

"Listen, fellas. I don't want you to miss this. You will never even enter heaven (much less be great) unless you change and become like little children."

RECALLING THE LITTLE GIRL IN ME

I have many fond memories of time spent with my mother when I was a child. One of my favorite memories is of mother-daughter trips downtown to the J.L. Hudson's where I did my "Christmas shopping". J.L. Hudson's was a huge department store famous for its Christmas displays, and its seasonal store created especially for children to shop for Christmas gifts while their parents shopped in the "big people" store.

At some point, during the Christmas season, we boarded the city bus and headed towards downtown. When we arrived at J.L

Hudson's my mother checked my coat, led me to the children's store, handed me a few dollars and dropped me off at the door. Parents were not allowed in the children's store.

The adult assigned to accompany me led me away from my mother. Never once did I think my mother would not return for me. I trusted the lady who helped me because I trusted my mother, who handed me over to the lady's care. I knew I had enough money for my gifts because my Mom made sure I had everything I needed. I shopped. I played. I enjoyed every moment. After an hour or so, my mother returned. I was usually hungry by the time she picked me up, but was never concerned about where we would eat. My mother took me to lunch. At the end of our day, we boarded the bus to return home, where I wrapped gifts, had dinner, and went to sleep.

That little girl trusted the one charged with her care. She did not worry about anything. A new adventure awaited her every day. She asked questions and learned. She trusted and obeyed. She depended and relished in the freedom dependence upon a trustworthy parent brought to her life. Young Cheryl never felt the need to make something happen. She didn't have to push. She asked. Every yes was celebrated. The word "no" wasn't always understood. Certainly, not liked. But, "no" was an acceptable answer to a little girl who felt loved and worthy.

The Cheryl who sobbed into her hands while sitting on the couch at 38 years old was just as much a loved daughter then as she was at the age of 5. And not just by the mother who asked her to change a light bulb.

CALLING THE LITTLE GIRL IN YOU

It is very hard to maintain childlike abandon and trust in a world which brings non-childlike pressure to bear on our hearts. A world which courts skepticism and self-protection in a culture which rewards doing and independence, and values self above anything else. With complete awareness and intimate knowledge of the backdrop of this world, Jesus requests us to release striving, and embrace again the security and freedom of dependent trust.

The day I lost it on the couch was probably the best day of that year. I had cannibalized my strength with self-reliance. The more I relied on me, the harder I pushed away God's guiding hand; and the weight of independence had consequences beyond my own sense of distance between me and the Lord. I had been snappy, fault-finding, and fighting overwhelm and exhaustion for weeks. Can you believe none of that nasty behavior registered with me?

The urgency of my depletion was overlooked as I sinned against my Father and those around me. My response to my mother's simple request finally shook me to the point of recognizing something was seriously wrong. Life had gotten in the way of living. I was merely existing with a parched, malnourished heart. Trying to get it done without the steady overflow of joy, grace, and strength from God's wellspring of life.

That day I began to recover what I had lost. During my recovery period I learned to drink deeply from the reservoir of God's living water; His Holy Spirit. I worshipped and prayed. I received sound counsel. I created much needed margin in my life for play. I wish I could tell you I completely obliterated the compulsion to strive. No. But, I did learn to depend more deeply on God, and His presence refreshed my soul. He never leaves us in a deprived state.

As we work our way through this first section, The Famished Heart, we will devote time to four key characteristics indicative of a malnourished heart; fearful, offended, hopeless, and weary. You will hear stories of people who struggled in these areas. You will learn how to overcome these specific obstacles to loving before being loved. Mostly, you will encounter thirst-quenching truth to irrigate your heart and light your way back to childlikeness in Christ

A HEART IN HIDING

How old were you when you first discovered God had a specific plan for your life? The first time you knew, without a doubt, He had a unique purpose for you? The "thing" for which you are a perfect fit and would joyously do even if you were never paid for it. It's okay if you haven't. Some of us never experience that "knowing." Most of us stumble our way into it. I got the first taste of it when I was 11 years old.

"Have you ever felt like you were supposed to do something great for God?"

I sat on the front porch with my mom in the cool of a summer evening. I can picture her, dressed in a blue outfit, leaning on the porch bannister. I was sitting in a chair, swinging my legs back and forth.

My mother responded, "Have I ever felt like you were supposed to do something great for God?"

"No, have you ever felt like you were supposed to do something great for God? Just in general."

"Not me. I have felt like you were. Why do you ask?"

"Because I feel like that. Like I'm supposed to do something great for God, but I don't know what that is."

I went on to college, then seminary, became a missionary, and led evangelistic crusades wherever God sent me. Now, in the latter half of life, I am writing books on the lessons learned from a life lived on the mission field.

Oh, the satire of it all! If only that were the case. Instead, I signed up for the Joseph Bar Jacob cruise to purpose.

FAVOR CONFERRED; FUTURE CONFIRMED

You know the story of Joseph, right? It's found in the book of Genesis, chapters 37 – 50. Joseph was the son of Jacob, who was renamed Israel, and whose 12 sons, one of whom was Joseph, became the forefathers of the tribes of Israel. Joseph was Jacob's favorite.

Joseph was born in Jacob's old age. As the oldest biological son of Jacob's favorite wife, Rachel, Jacob doted on Joseph. It was apparent to all the brothers, who worked in the fields under the blistering sun while Joseph remained at their father's side. If that wasn't bad enough, Jacob bestowed upon his beloved son a cloak made from strips of dyed cloth sown together.

That Joseph had a cloak was not the issue. All of the brothers had cloaks. It was the choice of colors in the cloak which made the gift problematic. It was very costly to create dyes. The colors chosen for Joseph's cloak more so. Vivid colors like red and purple were especially valuable. The coat was over-the-top for a nomadic tribe of shepherds. It was an expensive gift, a badge of preeminence for the preferred son. With this gift, Jacob made it clear, in no uncertain terms, who would be the recipient of his legacy if he had a choice. First in his eyes. First in his heart. The gift definitely fueled the brothers' jealousy. However, things didn't go south for Joseph until he began sharing God's greater purpose for his life.

Joseph had a series of dreams in which he saw his family bowing before him. Joseph shared those dreams with his family. I can't quite figure out if he was blind, naïve, or arrogant. His dreams did not sit well with brothers who were "over it" with the fawning Joseph received from their father. Joseph's antagonists were ignited. They were ready to be rid of this "daddy's boy." Kill him. The plotting began.

I recognized a sense of destiny for my life early on. Like Joseph, I too, had a God-given dream. While in college, I had a vision of myself, in front of thousands of women speaking to them about something I did not know in real life, at the age of 18. An older version of myself, stood on a back-lit stage, ministering to a crowd of beloved sisters about the grace of God accomplishing in and through them what they could not do on their own. I can tell you what I wore, how my hair was styled, and how I moved. It was vivid. Like a coat of many colors.

When we became Christ followers, we were adopted into the family of God (Romans 8:15). We are daughters. Daughters with a conferment of acceptance. Daughters with a God-planned future. As adopted daughters, our Father has bestowed upon your life, and mine, His multi-hued badge of sonship: wholeness, favor, peace, joy, righteousness, belonging, purpose, and most of all, Himself. It's a commendation of our value to Him; indicative of His great love, and our privileged position in His heart.

God has a dream for your life. A purpose. A reason for which you were created and brought to this juncture in your life. I'm sure not only do you want to know what it is, but you want to fulfill it. I sure did. I'm sure Joseph did as well. But, when you have a lion on your scent, the direct route is not the one you travel.

As you read through the last third of Genesis, you will find it was a long winding road for Joseph. His journey toward the "good" God had in store for him seem roadblocked by the betrayal and lies of his antagonists. He was thrown into a pit, then sold into slavery. He was falsely accused of attempted rape by his "master's" wife, then thrown into prison. There he both languished and prospered. They sometimes go hand-in-hand. He interpreted dreams for others while his own remained unrealized. His antagonists could not have planned for a more bitter end.

We have an antagonist. A jealous, deceitful, plotting antagonist, whose lust for our demise is unparalleled to anything else. He hates us. He hates our relationship with the Father. And, like Joseph's brothers, he salivates at the thought of our annihilation. He walks around, like a roaring lion, waiting for the opportunity to pounce on unsuspecting prey.

DREAMS DEFERRED

I lost my way somewhere between the age of 11 when I was sure of God's purpose in my life, and age 16 when I went to college as a rudderless young woman. Around age 12 I became acutely aware of the opposite sex, and just as acutely aware of the physical differences between me and other girls. The first obstacle was erected. Suddenly differences became deficiencies and I was not pretty enough. But, one thing no one could take away from me was my intelligence. I was pretty smart.

I went to a magnet high school for the academically gifted. Just one of hundreds of other students. Grades usually came very easy for me, but now I had to work for them. I remember the first time I got a "B" on my report card. Some of my other friends got straight "A's". There was an asterisk next to their name on the posted honor roll. The absence of my asterisk signaled I was not smart enough. The second obstacle was erected.

Each and every time I embraced a lie, darkness deepened around my heart until I was not sure who I was or what I wanted. At the time, it never occurred to me to ask God for His help and direction. I went to the college I attended because my friend was going there. I chose my major because my friend chose it. I married my first husband when I did because he didn't want to wait until I finished undergrad and grad school. Everything I chose was based on the desires of others. My heart was in hiding. Even from myself.

I was afraid. Afraid to own failure. Afraid to own success. Afraid of challenge. Afraid of tedium. Afraid to be seen, afraid of invisibility. I desired so much that I was afraid to pursue anything; especially intimacy with God, His purpose, and a deeply connected marriage. Too much of my life remained under the control of an amateur: me. I became acutely aware of the yawning ache in my heart but refused to voice the changes I wanted for fear of being stuck with unmet needs. I was at an impasse. We will struggle to experience God's perfect will if we live in fear of what may happen.

Fear is a powerful game changer. It challenges hope. It fights against ability and reason. It's a sickness that infects and causes deadlock where there should be progress. Fear chokes, fear denies, fear obscures truth. Fear keeps you from living and keeps your heart trembling behind unlocked prison doors.

About a year before everything went haywire in our home, I said to my first husband, "I am not going to be the same person this time next year that I am today!" I had reached the end of my rope, No more living with a closed-off heart. Ten months after that declaration I lost one of my dearest friends to complications arising from cancer treatment. We prayed, fasted, believed, and declared. She died. Like Joseph, I was thrown into a pit of despair. Questioning God. Questioning life. Questioning His plan. His dream for my life was the furthest thought from my mind. One morning, two months after she died, I woke up at 3:00 a.m. and "heard" these words impressed upon my heart, "Something is coming to attack your marriage." I went from the pit to the prison.

What followed was two years of craziness I cannot describe here...but the Cheryl which emerged from the prison is the Cheryl which had been hidden all those years! I could not be the same. God led me into the storm, ushered me through the storm, and used that tumultuous time to reshape me. He stripped away layers of lies, self-deception, self-lordship, and more. He tenderized my heart, and created beauty from the ashes. When all was said and done, I could say, like Joseph, what my antagonist meant for evil, God used for good.

COSTLY FEAR

My first brush with love was both exhilarating and agonizing. My inexperienced heart soared every time I doodled "Mr. & Mrs. Blah-Blah" on the paper in my notebook. The hearts and squiggly lines I added bolstered my romantic notions. Sadly, my 6th grade crush never reciprocated my intense feelings for him. Teenage crushes came and went. Young love flared and fizzled. The rejection stung quite a bit then. Today, I look back with fondness and humor.

It wasn't until I was in college that I "fell in love" for real. That man became my husband. We married in 1987, had our only child, a daughter, in 1993, were "in love" for 15 ½ years, before he "fell out of love" and ended our marriage after 17 years.

I realize in hindsight neither he nor I were "all in" in our marriage. I couldn't be. Married at 18, a junior in college, I became a "we" before I was a "me." How could I offer what I didn't yet understand? He couldn't be all in. He hid a deep need for constant validation, to be seen as heroic. Dating partners became props to boost his ego. Rather than work through difficulties in relationships, he jettisoned the person who no longer made him feel good, often already involved with his "new love" before ending the previous relationship. A pattern which repeated itself when he and I began dating, as well as in our marriage. Both children of broken relationships, we did not have an up close and personal example of how to work together to have a marriage infused with a love that surpassed feelings and overcame challenges.

My first husband and I resided in fear. We prayed, read the word, and were in ministry together. We talked, laughed, and made love. Still, we did not completely trust the other with our hearts. We did not let go. I disappointed him because I could not fit into the mold he created for me. He disappointed me because he could not fulfill my need for affirmation. We feared failure, yet we feared connection. We wanted to succeed, yet we divorced.

Rather than welcome openness and intimacy, fear kept us locked in competition, our hearts hidden from each other. Vulnerability became an enemy for fear of being hurt. Fear of not being heard silenced our authentic voices. Fear of being ridiculed, or diminished, kept us from reaching for each other. Fear of losing kept us from winning.

Our hearts needed continuous coaxing to come out of hiding. Eventually we wore each other out. And we each, in our own way, attempted to use the excuses for our divorce to absolve ourselves from the responsibility we had to move beyond fear and love each other, and our daughter, and Jesus, enough to fight for our marriage.

Fearing hearts hide, and hidden hearts are stingy hearts. There is no unabated love gushing from a heart hidden behind walls, loaded down with caution, sarcasm, and mistrust. I yearned for something different. Perhaps you do as well. Do you find yourself longing to experience freedom down in your soul? Not merely give mental assent to Christ setting you free, but, know the wild liberation of being in Christ? Free of hesitation. Free of habits and behaviors which keep you safe but unknown.

For my own sake, and that of all my relationships, I abandoned myself to the Potter's wheel. I became desperate to interact with others and engage in the world as if I actually believed that I am "in Christ." I am desperate to do the same today. And, much like Joseph, you and I have Almighty God, patiently guiding us over the rough terrain of stuck places to wide open fields of grace. If we allow Him behind the walls, the Lord will destroy the suffocating anxiety and lies which safeguards insecurity, condemnation, and torment in our hidden hearts. He will immerse you into lavish, freeing, love. Are you ready to come out of hiding?

COAXED OUT OF HIDING

Love is something chosen. A choice accompanied by emotions but still, a choice. Every day. In good and difficult times alike. Whether locked in fear or freed in faith. Because, first and foremost, love is a Person, upon whom we have staked our eternity. That Person takes the question of emotion off the table:

Love is patient and kind. Love is not jealous, it does not brag, and it is not proud. Love is not rude, it is not selfish, and it cannot be made angry easily. Love does not remember wrongs done against it. Love is never happy when others do wrong, but it is always happy with the truth. Love never gives up on people. It never stops trusting, never loses hope, and never quits. Love will never end....
1 Corinthians 13:4-8a (ERV)

There it is. Agape love. Notice, not one mention of an emotion. With a complete lack of restraint, God's love throws out the welcome mat. Agape is so other-focused there is no room for self-protection. It's the barometer by which we measure whether we are truly loving others. Agape love, God's love, is brave and precarious, because it is unconditional. It factors in neither reciprocity, nor emotion. Agape makes a choice to stick because it believes and hopes all things. It makes a choice to be patient. To forgive. To not hold a grudge. Ever. Agape is resolute. It is risky because it is resolute. And if there's one thing a heart in hiding is, it's risk-averse.

I cried when the Lord began revealing how fear-driven my choices had been. I cried for lost opportunities, roads not taken, friendships not developed, choices not made. Regret is a harsh, unrelenting companion. Then I dried my tears and asked, "What now, Father?"

God's dream for Joseph came to pass. Joseph's family bowed before him, but it was an open-hearted Joseph to whom they bowed.

That Joseph pointed his family to the God who provides. God's dream for my life came to pass. I am writing and teaching. I have spoken to countless women and will continue to do so as long as He allows it. But it is an open-hearted Cheryl who stands before His daughters. That Cheryl points them to the God who loves them and provides everything needed.

MAKING MOVES

The first step in learning how to love before being loved is to bring that heart out of hiding. For me, exposing my heart came on the heels of a painful circumstance. At that point, I had nothing to lose. I had gone the route of protecting my heart and still the worst happened. I let go, surrendered, and gave the care of my heart back to the only One who could care for it in the first place.

Along the way, I discovered a few things:

◊ The more open you are, the more likely you'll get hurt, but it's way better than remaining isolated within relationships.

◊ God is a better protector of our heart than we could ever hope to be. When it gets stung, and yes, that will happen, we can take that pain, discouragement, and upset attitude, right to Abba. He will comfort us.

◊ We won't always feel affectionate, but it's important we keep doing love. The emotions will catch up at some point.

◊ Eventually fear loses its grip. Apostle John reminds us in 1 John 4 there is no fear in love for perfect love drives out fear (1 John 4:18). Keep your heart accessible to the people in your life while God is working in it. Fear will go.

◊ We don't have to rely on our own reservoir of love. The love of God, 1st Corinthians 13 love, has been poured into our hearts by the Holy Spirit (Romans 5:5). When our emotional tanks are running on empty, the Holy Spirit will refill and strengthen us.

◊ As you uncover your heart, God does the work of recovering it. He heals, redeems, restores, and writes truth upon your heart.

It is the Father's delight to give us the Kingdom along with all of the benefits which come from being His daughters. We are not alone. We don't even have to do the heavy lifting. Trust God to do what only He can do.

Paul wrote the following to the church in Corinth:

Now it is God who makes both us and you stand firm in Christ. He anointed us, set his seal of ownership on us, and put his Spirit in our hearts as a deposit, guaranteeing what is to come.
2 Corinthians 1:21-23

Those of us who place faith in Jesus Christ for salvation, and yield to the Lordship of Christ in our daily lives, have a promise from a Guarantor who has never welched. His companionship guarantees help and belonging for today, and life for eternity.

The invitation to confident, open-hearted living is contained within that guarantee; if it only gets better from this moment, we can live unafraid in this moment. We can take off the masks and unveil our hearts.

I emerged slowly out of hiding. During the process I prayed, a lot. I talked, listened, and meditated on God's word. Inconsistency was my travel buddy. I back-tracked, reverted, moved forward, and got better. There were many "oops" even as my mind was renewed by truth. I began to act and think differently but much like a baby taking those first teetering, tentative steps, I fell quite a bit.

When I began to speak honestly from a heart no longer tethered to fear and people pleasing it was off-putting to some around me. My long dormant, God-given dreams resurfaced as I admitted my need for purpose and significance. Hope sprung to life as I discovered it was okay to open up. Scary, but okay.

WALKING THROUGH OPEN DOORS

I had a choice to make. "Will you love them like your own?" The pace of my heart quickened. My breath caught. I felt the need to remove my shoes. I stood on holy ground as the Father courted submission. Could I say, "yes?" Should I? "Yes" meant exposure. I knew I would be opening myself up to rejection, conflict and misjudgment. I wasn't only saying yes to becoming Jonathan's wife. I was saying yes to loving my bonus children with the same love Christ shows to all of us. Even today my hands tremble with the enormity of what He asks of me. Living with an open heart sounded wonderful in theory. Was God's strength enough? With small confidence and a lot of hope, I said, "yes," to God. That was the exact moment my relationship with one of my bonus children became a bit more difficult.

We were held prisoners to conflict of loyalties, a very normal stepfamily dynamic. Webs of mistrust, friction, and distress wove throughout our relationship. She wrestled with finding a way to enjoy a growing relationship with me without feeling like she was betraying her mom. I wrestled with staying consistent while dealing with changing and challenging moods. We each failed miserably at times. I was determined to not withdraw, or hide, or withhold. But how do you know when you're still in hiding?

If you recognize defensiveness in your interactions with your stepchildren, you may have a heart in hiding. If you are withholding affection, you may have a heart in hiding. If, instead of taking measures to remove yourself from toxic behavior, you harden your heart against rejection, you may have a heart in hiding.

This is not God's will for you. He desires our healed, whole hearts to fill up on His strength and grace, love lavishly and walk in victory in our families. Strut right on up to closed-hearts and watch His consistent love open them wide.

How you come out of hiding will depend on a few things:

◊ What's cloaking your heart? Is it fear? Childhood trauma? Abandonment? Rejection? Some issues may be prayed through or worked through with a wise and trusted friend. Others may require the assistance of a skilled therapist.

◊ How hidden is your heart? Are you very self-aware but choosing to remain closed off? Do you have a hard time identifying your feelings? Distinguishing between perspective and truth? Perhaps it would be helpful to ask yourself some questions when reacting to a situation: "Why is this bothering me? What wound is this situation triggering?" It might be time to expand your emotional vocabulary beyond the basics of happy, sad, angry, etc.

◊ Are you ready for the long haul? It will take time to reach the destination. Prepare for long-term engagement with your heart. Of course, God can, and sometimes will, circumvent natural processes with supernatural intervention. However, He often uses time to grow our character as He heals our emotions.

◊ What learned behaviors are you using to protect your heart? Sarcasm? Put-downs? Self-deprecation? Notice what makes you uncomfortable and what you do to deflect that unrest. When you become mindful of these behaviors, you're more likely to change them.

◊ How often is your heart assaulted? Are you living in a constant battleground? It is harder to expose your heart in tension and strife.

◊ How desperate are you to be free of your self-imprisonment? Is this a non-issue for you? Are you comfortable with the status quo and unwilling to upset the apple cart? Or are you ready to do whatever it takes to have better?

I would not be a good sister if I didn't tell you that living with an open heart requires just as much work as coming out of hiding.

I had done quite a bit of solo work, by the time Jonathan and I married but some uncovering is accomplished only within the context of a relationship. Healing enough to marry again was a big step for me. An even deeper work began when I became a stepmom. My love for Jonathan was willingly reciprocated. That was not necessarily the case with my new children. Would I be able to keep my heart open when rejected? Challenged? Misunderstood? When my daughter was hurt by a careless word or thoughtless action?

Although it's easier, I still have to work at keeping my heart unhidden. My default when hurt or offended is to retreat and withhold. I have learned to manage exposure by staying hidden in Christ. I run to His truth when rejection, my own, and especially that of my daughter's, rears its ugly head and my heart makes a case for retreat. I embrace His perspective of my worth and value when I feel ashamed or excluded. The Holy Spirit has taught me to pause and wait for His strength when weakened by my own failing efforts to deal with the dynamics in which we live.

We are not encouraged by Jesus to feel a certain way. Feelings of affection, trust, a sense of belonging, and the like, will need time to develop, along with a consistent deposit of positive interactions. Love, however, can be shown from the onset, and persistent love will create the environment in which affection, trust, and friendship can grow. We can choose.

I once read a quote listing juxtaposing circumstances, declaring each to be hard; "Marriage is hard. Divorce is hard. Obesity is hard. Staying fit is hard." The quote then encourages the reader to choose your hard. Everything has some level of difficulty attached to it. Loving your stepchild before they love you back is hard. Remaining withdrawn in relationship with them is hard. Pick wisely. Choose which outcome is worth the difficulty. It will be difficult. You've developed habits which make you feel safe behind those walls. It's a false security, but still, the first few steps away from that illusion will challenge you.

Do the work to bring your heart out of hiding. True, a revealed heart is more vulnerable, but a hidden heart will keep you from the purpose of your role in the lives of your stepchildren: to provide another taste of God's goodness and intentional love for them and make Him known to each one.

TREASURE HUNT

Alright sisters, it's time to go on a little adventure. Grab your tools, namely your bible, journal, and pen, and let's do a little digging.

1 Thessalonians 2:7-8 reads:

> Instead, we were like young children among you. Just as a
> nursing mother cares for her children, so we cared for you.
> Because we loved you so much, we were delighted to share
> with you not only the gospel of God but our lives as well. (NIV)

We glean a deeper meaning from the Amplified Classic translation: But we behaved gently when we were among you, like a devoted mother nursing and cherishing her own children. So, being thus tenderly and affectionately desirous of you, we continued to share with you not only God's good news (the Gospel) but also our own lives as well, for you had become so very dear to us.

Reread 1 Thessalonians 2: 1-8.

How does your heart attitude toward the children gifted to you through marriage compare to that of Paul's towards the Thessalonians? What is God revealing to you about your thoughts towards your bonus children? Are they pleasing to Him?

Ask God to give you His eternal perspective on your role in your family. Ask Him to work love and affection for your family into your heart, so that you can give them both the Gospel and yourself. Trust that He will complete this work in you.

SHARK BAIT

Author, Seth Godin wrote: "The problem with taking offense is that it's really hard to figure out what to do with it after you're done using it. Better to just leave it on the table and walk away. Umbrage untaken quietly disappears." He may not know it, but that's a noble and godly position to take on offense.

Samantha sat across the table trying very hard to suppress her heartache. She failed. Her bubbly personality was dulled by emotional turmoil. Her efforts to appear at ease stunted the flow of conversation. When her friend could no longer deal with the false note in Samantha's tone, she leaned in, looked at Samantha and said:

"Sam, don't you think it's time you told me what's going on?"

RARE AIR

The best part of a conversation for me is the pause between shallow, quick answers and the honest answers which need time and encouragement to surface. A tangible shift occurs, and pressure mounts, as the person across the table vacillates between caution and courage. In these moments, I resist the temptation to fill the silence. Authenticity can't be rushed. It's wooed with safety and acceptance. If we wait long enough, the peace of God fills that space, creating rarefied air where masks are replaced with genuineness.

The next words Samantha says are, "Can I be honest with you?"

For far too long I was satisfied with surface talk. It is quite convenient to stay away from someone's disturbing "life stuff." My day can continue in an uninterrupted focus on "my stuff" when I accept a quick "I'm fine," but you and I miss out when we rush past people God wants to reach.

We are gifts God gives to each other. Our presence, prayers, and listening ears, are cups used to bring cool refreshment to each other. Sam needed patient regard until she could release anxiety and confusion.

Her friend took a deep breath, and replied, "Yes." They bravely crossed the chasm between chatter and connection.

LOVE, OR SOMETHING LIKE IT

Samantha and her husband had five children between them, a "yours, mine and ours" combination ranging in ages 3 to 15 years old. In their seven years as a family, they experienced the usual ups and downs of living in step. Mostly ups. The birth of three-year-old Micah gave them a deeper connection as they bonded over their shared love for the new baby in the family. Overall, Samantha felt her family was well on their way to being a healthy unit. With one exception: Renee, Dave's 14-year-old daughter from his first marriage. She was the reason for Samantha's tentative, "Can I be honest with you?" request.

Samantha took a long sip of tea, using the time to gather her words.

"I love Dave. I love our family. I even love Renee. At least, I think I do. She is just so moody and messy and nasty; it's hard to like her. I could chock it up to being a teenager but she's always been that way towards me. Now she's even acting out with Micah. When he was an infant, she would snuggle with him, rock him to sleep. I thought there was hope. Then all of a sudden, two years ago, there was an abrupt about face and she's worse than ever. If it wasn't constant, I could deal with it, but every time she's with us there's so much tension and meanness in the house. It's much better when she's not there. I really just wish she would stay away!"

Tears began pooling in her eyes, her hands started shaking. Clearly in distress, Samantha continued,

"It's been 7 years. I just want to see an inkling of change. Anything! Can you imagine 20 more years of this? Dealing with her ruining holidays and vacations? I don't even wanna [sic] think about the show she and her mom will put on for her wedding!"

Samantha went on to describe, in minute detail, incident after incident of mistreatment she'd suffered at Renee's antics. Her heart was shredded. Torn apart by hurts, insults, disrespect, and hostility. Sam wanted to love Renee. She could only manage to tolerate her. Barely. She was unwillingly cordial with Renee. Too repulsed for anything but resentment. Sam wasn't wrong. Renee's behavior needed to be reined in. Sam had every right to be upset. However, she was far beyond upset. She was offended. She had a few things working in her favor, however. Samantha desperately wanted to be free from offense. She possessed an overwhelming desire to please God. Samantha invited the Lord to do a work in her heart, and you know our Father: He never refuses a sincere invitation to remodel a heart in which He lives.

CHUMMING THE WATER

I can ask a question to which I'm sure every shark enthusiast reading this knows the answer. What happens at the end of July? Shark Week: the longest running television summer event! I set my calendar for Shark Week. Raise your hand if you're with me. Shark Week is not Shark Week without at least one feeding frenzy scene. A feeding frenzy occurs when multiple sharks zero in on a single wounded prey. The wounded animal's blood in the water is like clanging the dinner bell and sharks answer the call. In droves. Sharks have different eating patterns. In sharks with distinct social structures, like hammerheads, big sharks eat first with leftovers going to smaller sharks. Whites are solitary sharks, living and eating alone or maybe coupled with one other shark. However, in feeding frenzies, a shark's usual pattern of behavior is overridden. They go in for the kill, caring little about social mores or need for space.

Movie makers use CGI (computer generated imagery) to simulate feeding frenzies on the big screen. To capture feeding frenzies on camera in real life, documentarians need more help than Hollywood movie magic can provide. Rather than leave a scene-making frenzy to chance, researchers will often ask their dive crew to chum the water. In order to draw sharks to the desired location, the crew will drop shredded, bloody, shark bait in the water near an area sharks are known to frequent.

The enemy of our soul is cunning and actively opposed to God's desires for our lives. His goals are to steal peace from us, kill our faith, and destroy our physical body and testimony, if he can (John 10:10). He accomplishes his goals primarily by distracting us from God's truth, goodness, and sovereignty. He has had millennia upon millennia to study mankind. He is neither all-powerful nor all-knowing, but he has gathered enough intel on the human race to wreak havoc in his limited capacity. One of his most effective weapons of choice is offense.

What makes offense proficient at derailing our walk with Christ? Dividing families? Starting wars?

Offense cuts, leaving us wounded and bleeding, ready for consumption, like chum in the water. The insults damage our dignity, luring enemies drawn by harsh feelings. The scent of offense reaches for nearby predators, inviting them to feast on our hope in God, our belief in His word, our family, our purpose, and our future. Offense readies our hearts to house predators like self-pity, resentment, bitterness, and unforgiveness. Offense tempts us to renounce God's ways. It is a most effective weapon.

John Bevere writes in *The Bait of Satan: Living Free from the Deadly Trap of Offense*:

> "A pure heart is like pure gold—soft, tender, and pliable. Hebrews 3:13 states that hearts are hardened through the deceitfulness of sin! If we do not deal with an offense, it will produce more fruit of sin, such as bitterness, anger, and resentment. This added substance hardens our hearts just as alloys harden gold. This reduces or removes tenderness, creating a loss of sensitivity. We are hindered in our ability to hear God's voice. Our accuracy to see is darkened. This is a perfect setting for deception."

Offense opens the door to Satan. It creates a clear pathway for the enemy to prevail in our lives. In effect, when we, adopted daughters of God hold on to offense, we bow before Satan. Unforgiveness, the retention of offense, enshrines Satan as the new lord of our lives. What a horrific thought!

Samantha's language, tone, even her facial expressions, were strident with bitterness. Anger escalated with each recounting of Renee's misdeeds. Offense had Samantha in its grip. It shredded her heart, and it wasn't finished.

OFFENSIVE OVERFLOW

If you ever watch a feeding frenzy, check the water after the sharks have eaten their fill. The area is replete with bits of carcass and blood; polluting the water as it floats away or sink to the bottom. The sharks indulging in chum create their own chum. It's the same with offense.

Samantha wasn't aware but harboring offense created a brokenness in her soul which leaked into other relationships. During the conversation at the table, she related several cringe worthy interactions she had with her husband. Small things, which someone with a good sense of humor would overlook, set off a 24-hour silent treatment from Samantha. She snapped at people at work and raged at drivers on the road. She was snarky with the waiter because he innocently forgot to bring straws to the table.

Offense is not content to remain within the heart of the offended. Its nature is to travel from an injured person to a new target. If we do not deal with offense, we will become offenders. We will pollute the lives and souls of people around us with pain.

THE REMEDY

Paul wrote to the church in Corinth, and to us today;

> Anyone whom you forgive, I also forgive. Indeed, what I have forgiven, if I have forgiven anything, has been for your sake in the presence of Christ, so that we would not be outwitted by Satan; for we are not ignorant of his designs.
>
> 2 Corinthians 2:10-11 (ESV)

Leading up to the verses above, Paul writes of an insult inflicted on him by a brother in Christ and the effect it had on the church. A man had confronted Paul with accusations from false teachers. Paul, motivated by his love for the church (v.4), wrote to encourage repentance from the man and those who agreed with him so that when he visited again, they would be able to enjoy fellowship in unity (v. 3). After the church dealt with the offender, Paul wrote again to encourage mercy.

The discipline the church at Corinth meted out was enough. Now, it was time to reaffirm the man through their love (v. 6-8). Paul ends this part of his letter by asserting his forgiveness of the offender. Paul reminded the offended congregation that his forgiveness was for the sake of the church in the presence of

Christ, who knows everything: "...so, that we would not be outwitted by Satan; for we are not ignorant of his designs." Paul was acutely aware that offense is a potent weapon in our enemy's arsenal. He refused to make it easy for the enemy to succeed.

Scripture encourages us to acknowledge hurt and disappointment. We honor our relationships when we lovingly and firmly speak up against offense and deal honestly with anger. Yet, our obedience is incomplete unless we forgive, each and every time we're offended. All the more if we are consistently offended by the same person. We are encouraged because allowing offense to fester in our hearts is a recipe for spiritual defeat. It is quite difficult to be both victorious in our walk with Christ and offended with others. The two are incompatible.

Many years of my life were hampered by offense and unforgiveness. I endured perpetual contempt and put-downs by a broken person. That's not an exaggeration. There was acute, deliberate, and repeated abuse from this person and every time she acted against me, I was sliced by offense again. I tried to overlook it but the unending assault wore me down. Eventually, unintentionally, I became an offender. I was touchy and self-protective. Perhaps it would be better to call it "flesh-protective." Always looking for someone to hurt me, I became a defensive, proud person. I could not love freely and without love we are not victorious. I was a sounding brass, a tinkling cymbal, making noise but having no real impact beyond the hurt feelings in my wake of impatience, insensitivity, and huffiness.

Thankfully God does not silently stand by, watching us flounder at following Him. He generously helps, reveals, and heals. He waits only to hear our cry, "Father, I need you!"

During a time of upheaval in my life, partly sustained by this same woman, I drew close to the Lord and He drew close to me. I cried, "Father, I need you!"

Amazingly, it was then, in the middle of turmoil, I grabbed hold of the ability to forgive. My eyes were opened. God has been very gracious to you and me, not holding our egregious sins against us. His grace taught me how to forgive and let go of offense while keeping healthy boundaries. In dying to self and laying down my right to be repaid for what I endured, I came alive to Christ in me, the hope of glory.

Some years later, on the heels of a tragic event, I had occasion to visit her at the nursing home where she resided. I entered her room and she stared at me for a few moments. The very first words she uttered were, "Cheryl, I'm sorry for everything." I was able to truthfully reply, "I forgive you." Praise God! There was no lingering animosity. By His grace, I had already forgiven her.

Our fight to love while we're waiting to be loved is not exclusively a fight for our families. Yes, we fight for the vision God has for our families. We fight for the integrity of our walk with Christ. We fight for the salvation of those watching, and for the bequeathing of our hearts and lives to the Lordship of Jesus Christ. We fight to maintain the hard-won freedom Christ has given to us. But that's not where our fight ends.

Our fight to love while we're waiting to be loved is also a fight against the enemy. Against his tactics. Against deception. Against his plans for our loved ones. Against the lies he spins and the division he pitches. Against the poison of offense.

Stand strong. Fight. And don't back down. Any display of authority by the enemy is bogus. God has the final word. By no means do we engage the enemy lightly. Yet, neither do we engage him timidly. We fight in battles already won by Jesus Christ. We need only follow the script for victory.

Samantha was told,

"Sam, you know Renee is not yet mature enough to realize she's hurting you because she's hurt herself. But you are. Offense is setting a trap for you, and you're walking right into it. For your sake and for the sake of your family, I think it's time for you to try this God's way"

We find the following instructions from Jesus in Luke 17:

> Then He said to the disciples, "It is impossible that no offenses should come, but woe to him through whom they do come! It would be better for him if a millstone were hung around his neck, and he were thrown into the sea, than that he should offend one of these little ones. Take heed to yourselves. If your brother sins against you, rebuke him; and if he repents, forgive him. And if he sins against you seven times in a day, and seven times in a day returns to you, saying, 'I repent,' you shall forgive him." (v. 1-4)

The word offenses here is the Greek word, *skandala*. It's meaning implies a snare, stumbling block, an offense. Literally it is a stick upon which people placed bait to trap animals for consumption.

Offense is inevitable. We cannot escape this battle. Jesus said so. Just remember it is coming with an objective: to bait us into sin, to trip us up, and to cause us to fall so we can be more easily devoured. Forgiveness is the only remedy. It is not easy to forgive the first offense, much less the seventh in a day. Nonetheless, we must forgive. You and I need to know what to do with offense when it shows up.

A DEFENSE AGAINST OFFENSE

To fulfill our God-given call as our child's stepmom, we have to manage offense when it happens; as well as guard against it before it happens. Can you imagine what it would be like to remain steady and composed in the face of personal attack? To shake off irritation, hard feelings, and insults like shaking dust off your feet? When someone offends us, it's natural to want to retaliate. Natural, yet deadly. With repeat offenders, it is tempting to close the door to a bonded relationship. Tempting, yet fatal.

Thankfully, you and I have been given a new nature, born of the Spirit of God. We are no longer limited to the low-level thinking of the old nature. We are new creatures. We do not have to follow the dictates of the flesh. We have been freed from the bondage of sin and iniquity. We walk in the supernatural grace of God. His ability is at work in us to accomplish what we cannot accomplish on our own. He commands in Romans 12:21, "Do not be overcome by evil but overcome evil with good," and He enables us to obey this directive.

Friend, I know your bonus children, and perhaps others, have hurt you, have excluded you, have offended you. It's time to put on your battle gear and fight back, God's way. It's time to fortify your heart, make it less accessible and less responsive to the bait of offense.

5 ACTIONS TO GUARD AGAINST OFFENSE

◊ If someone were to shake my hand, I am unlikely to respond in any way other than by shaking their hand as well. But, if someone shakes my broken hand, I am going to scream. Typically, offense comes when we're triggered in a place of woundedness. Someone has shaken our broken place and we're screaming. Unfortunately, we often don't know what our wounds are or how they occurred. Take time to discover your story. Ask Jesus to help you see what wounds you may have and how they affect your ability to deal with offenses. If needed, enlist the help of your pastor or a good therapist to gain insight and healing.

◊ Shhh! Stop fighting. Erect and maintain healthy boundaries! Tear down your walls but keep your fences.

John Bevere writes in *The Bait of Satan: Living Free from the Deadly Trap of Offense*: "We construct walls when we are hurt to safeguard our hearts and prevent any future wounds. We become selective, denying entry to all we fear will hurt us. We filter out anyone we think owes us something. We withhold access until these people have paid their debts in full. We open our lives only to those we believe are on our side." Walls separate. In every way. Healthy boundaries, however, are the physical, emotional and mental limits we establish to protect ourselves from being manipulated, used, or violated by others while remaining open to them. They allow us to separate who we are, and what we think and feel, from the thoughts and feelings of others. The presence of healthy boundaries helps us express ourselves as the unique individuals we are, while we acknowledge and esteem the same in others.

◊ Determine beforehand to avoid the boxing ring. Proverbs 26:21 tells us, "*Just as charcoal and wood keep a fire going, a quarrelsome person keeps an argument going.*" Offense needs fuel to reach maximum effectiveness. Don't feed the beast. As much as it depends on you, walk in peace with all men. (Romans 12:18) Attack issues, not your stepchildren. Correct behavior without arguing about perspective.

◊ Manage your expectations so you will apply pressure in the appropriate place. There is a huge difference between good desires and lust. We were made for relationship with others. That is a good desire given to us by God. However, relationships with others were not made to fill all of our relational needs. To demand, or even expect someone to fulfill our relational longings, is lust and a form of idolatry. Only God has the capacity to provide for our emotional wholeness. Look to the Father for the deeper needs of acceptance, validation, identity, security, and emotional healing. This will make it easier for you to love the people in your life without pressuring them to love you in return and feeling offended when they cannot.

◊ I cannot emphasize this enough: spend time worshipping God. Maintaining a proper view of God will help you maintain a proper view of who you are. We serve a Holy God, without sin or stain, who is just in His offense at our sin. Rather than punish us, He removes our sin through the precious blood of Jesus. Forgiving the offenses of one sinner against another is easier when we consider that. That does not mean it will be effortless, but it is less painful when we realize how much we owe God.

All that being said, no matter how adept we become at guarding against offense, it will burst through those defenses at some point. I had to learn what to do when offended. If you are wondering how to reclaim peace when offended, I have something which may help:

5 ACTIONS TO RECOVER FROM OFFENSE

◊ Acknowledge your feelings. In the scriptures we read in Luke 17, Jesus instructed us: "...*If your brother sins against you, rebuke him...*" Recovering from offense in no way means denying you've been hurt. We're encouraged by Jesus to go to our "brother" (or sister, or husband, or whomever) and LOVINGLY rebuke their actions, in order to bring about reconciliation. Hurt feelings will not diminish with denial. They will only grow stronger. Deal with them quickly.

◊ Proverbs 19:11 reads, "A *man's wisdom gives him patience. It is to his glory to overlook an offense.*" Offense provides an opportunity for us to grow into greater glory. God does not waste anything. Offense is a tool for spiritual training. As we focus on His faithfulness rather than our hurt, God uses offense for our good: to change us to look, think, and act, more and more like Jesus. Give Him access to your heart when offended. He will help you overlook offense, causing you to mature in Christ.

◊ Don't wait for an apology. It may never come. Choose to forgive. Jesus asked the Father to forgive his executioners while He was dying. (Luke 23:34) Paul reminds us in Colossians, "You must make allowance for each other's faults and forgive the person who offends you. Remember the Lord forgave you, so you must forgive others." (Col 3:13) Holding on to an offense keeps you shackled to the wound, sets the stage for bitterness to take root in your heart, and, according to the Bible, results in God withholding His forgiveness (Matthew 6:15). Free yourself. Do not wait for relief or good feelings to return. Make allowances for others and choose forgiveness as often as you need to.

◊ "You even put up with anyone who enslaves you or exploits you or takes advantage of you or pushes himself forward or slaps you in the face." (2 Corinthians 11:20) As much as possible, remove yourself from repeat offenders. Value what God values. God values both you and the person who has hurt you. He values peace and unity. He values your family. He values justice. Removing yourself will give you the needed space to determine how to respond. Distance makes it easier to recover from offense through prayer and a renewed perspective. Ask yourself a question I learned from my friend, author, Summer Butler: Are you able to remain in relationship with the person and not act in sinful ways towards them because of their actions against you? If not, step away.

◊ Pray. Repeatedly. Forgiveness doesn't happen in one fell swoop; don't stop praying until you have totally forgiven the offender. Bring your authentic self to your time of prayer. I confess to God when it is hard for me to forgive, and I ask Him to help me obey Him. He always helps when we cry out to Him for assistance. After you have prayed for yourself, pray for the person who has offended you. Gulp! Ask God to bless them. Those you have hurt may be caught in the snare of offense. Pray for them. Ask God to remove the sting of the pain you caused and help them recover well.

With these, Samantha was armed to change the outcome of her interactions with Renee. Renee did not immediately change her behavior. Often, it felt like her behavior got worse. Samantha, however, was no longer a slave to offense. She was able to see offense for the trap it is and walk away. With God's help so can you.

Living in a stepfamily is the best training ground for learning how to not give in to offense. What a blessing of an opportunity we have! My beloved Sister, you're on a bullet train towards living unoffended. Not because offenses won't happen, but because our Father braces us against offenses so that they are not allowed to take root in our hearts. You will likely experience a baptism of fire into criticism, misunderstanding, and misrepresentation. Take heart. Your Heavenly Champion has given you the victory...live it out.

TREASURE HUNT

Alright sisters, it's time to go on a little adventure. Grab your tools, namely, your bible, journal, and pen, and let's do a little digging.

"But you, O Sovereign Lord, deal well with me for your name's sake; out of the goodness of your love, deliver me. For I am poor and needy, and my heart is wounded within me." Psalm 109: 21-22 NIV

Find a quiet spot and give yourself some time to be patient with our Treasure Hunt today. Think about an incident where you were particularly hurt by the words or actions of your stepchild. Take a moment to pray and ask Jesus to reveal deeper truths about yourself in context of your hurt. Ask yourself a few questions:

◊   What hurtful feelings were stirred?
◊   What past experiences do I associate with those feelings? What wounds were touched?
◊   What lies do I believe about myself because of those wounds?
◊   How did these past experiences shape my response to my stepchild?
◊   How might God be using this incident to help me live unoffended?

Now spend time in prayer over your discoveries. Specifically ask Jesus to give you the truth to combat every lie you believe.

HOPE DEFERRED

"How can I pray for you?"
That's the question I asked the young woman who, more than likely, had just finished "her date."

I work with an organization that ministers to people caught in the horrors of sex trafficking. Once a week we drive to a specified area, hand out toiletries, a packed lunch, and other items (coats, blankets, socks, shoes, umbrellas, gloves) as needed. Always we pray. For those who call the hotline number and say the words we all long to hear, "I want to get off the streets," we organize a safe house from which we rescue them, and take them to a rehab program, since, in all likelihood, they are battling a drug addiction. From there, they are sent to a life-skills program. After that, they are given a mentor for one year. I am part of the outreach team which dispenses food and toiletries, and also a mentor. We go to the same location every week. Our friends know us and we know them. Some of their family members are in touch with our organization. Always we pray.

I had not been long with the organization before I noticed something. There is a distinct difference between the man or woman who at least attempts to escape from that life and the one who has resigned him or herself to a life trapped in the chaos, objectification, and despair of sex trafficking. You can see it in their eyes. You can hear it in the lilt of the voice when you are asked to pray. The difference is hope; the expectation that something good can come from taking one step.

DEFINING HOPE

The prophet Jeremiah wrote, on behalf of the Lord, "I know the plans and the thoughts I have for you...thoughts and plans for welfare and peace, not for evil, to give you hope in your final outcome," (Jeremiah 29:11a). The Hebrew word for hope is *yachal*. It means to have a confident expectation, usually accompanied by pleasurable anticipation. Biblical hope is closer to faith than it is wishing. The Bible says that faith is the substance of things hoped for. Faith points hope like a laser. "Hope talk" sounds like this: "God, I thank You for providing for and meeting all of my needs according to your riches in glory." "Faith talk" sounds like this: "Lord, I thank you for providing for the mission trip to Puerto Rico." Hope is general confidence in God. Faith is focused confidence in God for a specific outcome. Both are gifts from God and are based upon His faithfulness to bring about His good plans for us.

I think the best definition I have found for biblical hope comes from the Dictionary of Bible Themes which defines hope as: "A total grounding of one's confidence and expectation in God's goodness and providential care even in the face of trouble." How does that sound to you? How would you like to live like that? To be able to say, "I am so convinced of the inevitable goodness of God being revealed in my life, I live in constant anticipation of that good, despite what I see going on around me!" Go ahead. Try it out on your tongue! See how it tastes. Tastes pretty good, doesn't it?

Real hope, biblical hope, has weight. It carries consequence and expectation. Hope turns a worrier into a warrior. Hope battles against self-sufficiency, silences doubt, celebrates in anticipation of what is to come. Hope rehearses God's track record of compassion, consistency, dependability, mercy, and favor, persuading us of future goodness coming our way from His loving hands. Hope has sharp teeth, making as short a meal of distrust and impatience as a pride of famished lions tearing into a wounded antelope. Hope is an anchor upon which stepmoms can wait well.

HEART SICK

Hope is powerful, which is why unrealized hope has great power. The Bible reads:

Unrelenting disappointment leaves you heartsick
Proverbs 13:12a (MSG)

The Hebrew word for sick is *challah*. It means to be weak or sick, severely wounded, afflicted. For stepmoms, being ignored, disrespected, and unloved by our husband's children sickens our hearts and robs us of hope. Pretending our hearts aren't hurting is not the answer for restoring hope. We will never find healing, nor will we acquire the freedom to love while waiting to be loved, if we don't attend to the ache inside.

What will it take to refill our famished hearts with hope? When there seems to be so few answers and only temporary relief for the twinges of isolation, loneliness, and fatigue that can plague a stepmom's hope? If hope is confidence, then hope should assure us those answers are already provided and will be made known in due time...at the right time.

WHEN A HERO COMES ALONG

One of my favorite interactions recorded in the Bible between Jesus and another individual is a confrontation He had with a woman whose name we do not know. Perhaps that's why I'm drawn to her story. She has no name, no identity. She is every woman and any woman. She could be me. She could be you. Like her, I have felt ostracized, as if I were the town pariah.

In John 4, we find Jesus travelling from Judea to Galilee. Although the quickest route to Galilee was to travel through Samaria, ancient Hebrews would travel north and then east to avoid "them".

Hebrews hated Samaritans, and Samaritans were not too fond of Hebrews. Their long-standing animosity was fierce. Any issue you may have with your spouse's former partner is nothing compared to these feuding cousins.

The Hebrews considered Samaritans half-breeds, less-than, not even good enough to be second-class citizens. They wanted nothing to do with Samaritans, even going so far as to add extra time and miles onto their travel to avoid one toe accidentally crossing into their land. Their very existence was a complete antithesis to the Hebrew way of life, yet the Samaritans rightfully claimed heritage as children of Abraham. Today, blended families are sometimes viewed as the exact opposite of what is good and normal to the Christian way of life, yet we, too, rightfully claim heritage as God's beloved chosen.

Jesus wanted to travel through Samaria. As a matter of fact, according to scripture, He said He *had* to go through Samaria (John 4:4). He was on assignment. We know there were other routes available to Jesus, but there was a reason for travelling through Samaria. We know "who" that reason was, too. She is simply called, "the woman at the well."

 It was an arduous journey, even though it was a shortcut. Hunger and thirst became unwelcomed travelling companions. Jesus and the disciples came upon a well in the Samaritan town of Sychar. It was Jacob's well; as in, "God of Abraham, Isaac and Jacob" Jacob. Jesus stopped at the well and set the scene. He sent the disciples away to get food, then sat down and waited. I can imagine Jesus' head leaned back against the stone, eyes closed, as the hot wind whisked the sweat from His brow. His hands, soon pierced for our sins, rested on His knees. He communed with the Father...as He waited.

A woman approached, alone. She carried buckets with which to draw water for her household. It is noon; the sun is at its peak. Women typically did not go to the well at noon. They drew water in the cooler parts of the day, usually the morning, not just because it was cool, but also because they needed fresh water for their families for the rest of the day.

The women of Sychar would likely travel in groups. They lived in a brutal society in which women were viewed as not much more than chattel. A woman would never travel alone to a well situated outside the safety of her community. She would want the protection of a group. Besides, we girls are very social. The women in Sychar would have gathered and travelled to the well together, chatting, laughing and catching up on the latest news along the way.

This woman made her way to the well by herself. It seems she did not know the enjoyment of sisterhood. No one loved her enough to provide even a token semblance of protection. Everything about this woman said she was deserted, unwanted, and unloved. This woman was an outcast, separated from her community because this woman was that woman. You know who that woman is...the talked about one. The one looked down upon. Can you sense her friendlessness? Are you familiar with her type of aloneness? Can you feel it leaping off the pages of the Bible, connecting with your heart? To cope with the exclusion, she pretends she is not lonely; that she doesn't care. Her laugh, and gaudy living, hides the hopelessness from all but the most astute. Jesus is the most astute.

The woman trekked through town, under the gloom of involuntary solitude, beat up by wagging tongues, and went to the well to draw her water. Why didn't she just leave the town and settle where no one knew her reputation? Perhaps she held out hope that things would change for her in the place she called home. Perhaps she wished for the day when she would be accepted by her neighbors. For whatever reason, she stayed and endured the rejection. Is that you today, my dear sister? Holding out hope that you will finally know love and acceptance in the place you call home? By all who live in your home?

She approached the well where a strange Hebrew man sat. Without preamble, He spoke: "Give me a drink." God makes the first move always. It is His kindness that draws us to repentance. It is His grace that makes salvation available. It is His gift of faith that makes it possible for us to believe. He meets us, where we are, and enters our world. He wants us to know the joy of fellowship with Him thus provides countless opportunities for us to see Him.

THE ROOM WHERE IT HAPPENS

Jesus spoke to her. In the Jewish custom, men were not allowed to speak to unrelated women in public. Particularly, He asked her to get Him a drink. Jesus did not have a cup from which He could drink. He had to drink from her cup; an act which would have made Him ceremonially unclean. He would have been unclean for some days, needing to go to the temple to make a sacrifice before He could be declared clean again. Jesus was well aware of this fact when He asked for a drink. Still, He asked. If that weren't enough, He deigned to speak to a Samaritan. The people the Jews despised. To even be seen speaking to a Samaritan was enough to make Jesus more of the outcast He was fast becoming.

When God determines to confront us with our need for Him, absolutely nothing will keep Him from doing so; not religious tradition, political affiliation, preconceived ideas, or the state of our family. Not anything. He is not confined to working in a way that makes us comfortable or to following rules we have put in place. Without losing a bit of His holiness, He steps right smack dab into the middle of our convoluted behavior, manipulating action, and self-medicating activity, cuts through the sludge, and deals with our hearts. At the appointed time, in the appointed place, Jesus will confront you.

She challenged Jesus with their differences. "How can you, being a Jewish man, ask me, a Samaritan woman for anything? Jews have nothing to do with us..." (John 4:9) Jesus was not there to engage in a fruitless debate. He cared about the woman behind the facade. "If you knew the gift of God standing before you, you would ask Him and He would give you living water." (John 4:10)

I will paraphrase her response, "You have nothing to draw with and the well is deep. How are you going to get this living water? Besides, don't you know whose well this is? This is Jacob's well. Are you greater than Jacob?" She sounds miffed. Jacob was revered in Israel. He was Israel, But, my goodness, God stood before her! She did not realize she was standing before the Answer to all of her questions. She attached reverence to the only thing that made sense to her at the time. How often have you clung to the familiar, although you hoped for more? How many times has God had to pry your hands loose from a thing which kept you from the real solution? For me, I can say far too many times to count. She's with Jesus; in the "room" where change can happen, yet she continued her devotion to tradition.

DRY UP OLD WELLS

To regain our hope, we must turn away from anything which has been unable to rekindle hope in our heart. We dip our buckets at Jacob's well when we look to people to feed our battered self-esteem, or activities and foods to release certain "feel good" chemicals in our bodies. We run to old wells when we value traditions, customs, and agendas over the presence of God. Familiarity is comforting. No matter how life-sucking our actions are, we stick with them because that's all we know. Unfortunately, we can quench the spirit of God, and miss the revival of hope, when we trust our wells more than His presence.

There are dry places in our stepfamilies. Arid places devoid of life. Opportunities for bonding, memory making, and more, lay dormant there, just waiting to be reawakened. Trying to get living water from dried up works, behaviors, and thinking, will not give us hope-filled lives. No matter how desperate we are, dry sources will not bring dry places back to life. There is no need to languish, trapped in a dry place. God's fresh, living water is within reach.

Unfortunately, much like this woman, we get offended when the Spirit of God challenges the effectiveness of our wells. We're dejected, tired of dipping buckets only to be left parched. Hope for our families is fading. Still, how dare anyone challenge the ability of old wells to give us revitalizing water!

When we are embroiled in hopelessness, reliance on what we know to do is no longer appropriate. The God who confronts our hopelessness, flips the script and says, *"Behold, I do a new thing! Now it shall spring forth, shall you not know it, I'll make a way in the wilderness and rivers in the desert..."* (Isaiah 43:19).

The wilderness is harsh and overgrown. No one tends to it. It is uncared for. Survival of the fittest is the law of the wilderness; eat or be eaten, kill or be killed. There is no easy source of fresh water. Only back-breaking effort will reach the water which might be deep in the earth. God, who through Jesus, exchanges our heavy yoke for His easy one, has better for us. In unyielding environments, like tense family situations, God makes a way of safe passage for you and me. He creates life-giving streams in a parched land.

Let go of those dried-up methods of trying to make something happen. All who enter the Kingdom can abandon the futility of self-dependent effort. Have hope. God will cause you to flourish, even in a dry place.

HE KNOWS YOUR TRUTH

I am always humbled and amazed by the wisdom in Jesus' response to people. In no way did Jesus acknowledge the woman's challenge. Instead, He addressed her need with, *"Those who drink that water will become thirsty again but those who drink the water I offer will not only not thirst again but a fresh bubbling spring will rise up in them giving them eternal life,"* (John 4:13-14).

She responded with, *"Sir, give me this water..."* Just when you are ready to cheer for her because you think, "She gets it," she continues, *"...so I don't have to come here and draw anymore."* (v. 15)

She did not say, "Give me this water so I can live." She said, "Give me this water and I won't thirst again. Then I will never, ever, have to come back to this place." Her raw hopelessness was on display in those words. Her focus was clearly on the emotional relief she felt was within reach. She wanted Jesus to alleviate the bitterness of rejection. She wanted cover for the shame. "Sir, make it so I don't have to deal with these folks anymore. I don't want to look at them and I don't want them looking at me."

I, too, have begged God for temporary relief while He offered a permanent solution. I uttered shortsighted prayers like, "God fix this so I don't have to deal with those folks." "Take this away so I don't have to feel this pain anymore!" I have pleaded, wished, and waited for the cavalry to arrive. "Give me this water so I don't have to come here again. They are hurting me and I'm tired of being shunned, rejected, and misunderstood!" Thankfully, He refused my requests for instant fixes. Instead, He offered redemption, recovery, and restoration.

God confronts us with our hopelessness, not to magnify our pain but to remind us that relief is not necessarily His objective. Our feelings are not immaterial, but there is something much bigger going on when God begins to peel back the layers of hopelessness.

His overall objective in confrontation is to unmask you; to set the stage where "real you" meets "real Him". The confrontation has nothing to do with the people causing us pain. I want problems fixed. He wants hearts transformed. The confrontation is about the relationship between the "confrontee" and the Confronter.

UNRAVELED

The child causing you the greatest anxiety right now is being used by the Lord to conform you into His image. The hopelessness you wrestle with is a springboard to realizing the joy of hope placed in God alone. The woman's relationship with the villagers, or the men she had been with, was not the topic at hand for Jesus.

Jesus, again not addressing the desire of the woman at the well but addressing the need, told her to go get her husband. She said, "I don't have one."

Finally, we're at the heart of the matter. At last, we are beyond religious masks, trivial debates, and requests for appeasement. "You've had five and the one you're with isn't yours." The unraveling begins.

There is nothing in our lives we need to hide from God, because there is nothing in our lives we can hide from God. There is no shame we bear of which He is not aware. Our secret thoughts are an open book to Him. There is nothing the dark can keep from the Father of Light. He knows everything about us. When God confronts us, the cards are already face up on the table. Can't you hear Jesus reaching out to the woman? Reaching out to you? "I know about the men. I know about the food...the pride...the spending...the withholding of love...I know! Now what? What objections do you have now? I see you and I'm still here. I know everything and I won't turn away. What obstacle is keeping you from Me? From My love for you? Let's deal with it, because I have life for you."

We avoid facing the truth about ourselves, but Jesus does not. He exposes our issues. Thank God! Only when all the crud we've used to hide behind is removed, can the real needs in our lives be uncovered and met. Anything hidden gains power. Exposure, however, diminishes shame, cripples strongholds, and lessens the burden of weights. He meets us where we are, and confronts our hopelessness, so we can be free. We thirst, He quenches. We starve, He nourishes. We have an infinite number of needs. He has a ceaseless supply of mercies. He is our hope.

We have been set free, but some of us are still bound by regret, sin, guilt, pain, pride, uncontrolled desires, and the need for validation. Like Lazarus, we have exited the tomb but remain wrapped in grave clothes. It is time to come unraveled. Jesus knows what you're hiding. He knows what you've done in order to feel accepted, to restore hope on your own. He witnessed your rejection of His life-giving water for the familiar. Desert that noxious, stale, water sitting in the deficient wells you've built. There's no life there. Jesus wants to give you hope.

THE CRUX OF THE MATTER

God helps us face our issues so He can deal with them. We do not get to play make believe any longer. We are sinners. Hopelessly lost without Him. Given to thinking ugly thoughts, and awful behavior. God brings hope where hope has long since died. God makes the old insignificant, giving us what is breathtakingly greater. He invites us to sit at the table and reason with Him. He lifts the stain of sin and the heaviness of infirmity. We become partakers of His holiness through Jesus Christ.

The woman at the well wanted to enter into a religious discourse. "I know that Messiah is coming" The answer is coming. "The Savior is on His way and when He comes, this is how we're supposed to worship Him." She was still drinking water from the well of religion, but Jesus kept redirecting her to truth. God has no stomach for religion. Relationship, yes; religion, no. Religion makes us comfortable with ritual, and keeps intimacy at arm's length. God wants to be up close and personal. Jesus hit her with a challenge to religion; "I AM."

Sometimes I get bold enough to ask God for a "Moses moment." "There's got to be more than this! I want to know You more. I want to see your Glory!" God said, "Yes" to Moses. God wants to be seen and known by His children. Jesus said to the woman; "I AM!" In other words, "Not only do I see you, but I want you to see Me. Not only do I know you, but I want you to know Me. I AM the Messiah! I AM the answer to your questions. I AM the solution to your problems. I AM the result of your seeking. I AM what you find on the other side of the door. I AM your hope. And, I AM more than enough!"

Finally! Here was the "aha" moment. She had come to the end of herself. She had no more objections, no more questions. It is fairly obvious she rediscovered hope. Look at her response. She ran back to the village, to the very people who gossiped about her, to the same men who shunned her and left her unprotected, to tell them she just met a man who told her all about herself and just may be the Messiah!

The love and acceptance we see when we gaze into the face of Jesus washes away the fear of rejection. There is nothing in Him that will not love us. His approval removes the sting of others' rejection. He fills our hearts with hope and we can't help but share that.

Now, filled with hope and joyful abandon, she ran to the village and announced, "Come meet a man...!" Hope lit up her eyes with evident change. Something in her tone and countenance captured their attention. This woman had known many, many men. Meeting another man was not news to her neighbors.

But, this Man?

"...who has told me all about myself!"

This one is different. He didn't take anything from me. He saw me. He poured into me. He restored my hope and joy!"

Now I don't have book, chapter and verse on this, so bear with me. I am using mere deductive reasoning, which is faulty at best. I believe it wasn't Jesus saying, "I know you've been with five men and the one you're with now is not your own," that restored her hope. That was mere confirmation of what was generally known. Yes, He pointed out her sin, but revealing sin without offering the remedy brings sorrow and condemnation, not hope. Her response indicates He did more than tell her what she, and everyone else, already knew. I believe He told her what she didn't know but had always prayed was true. I believe He told her who she was to Him. I believe He looked at her and said, "You are more than what you think!" I believe He restored her hope in God by seeing the cared for daughter beyond the outward mask of enticing clothes, heavy makeup, and multiple lovers. I believe He gave her a drink of Kingdom water and it quenched her thirst!

I believe He will do that for you today. As you abandon yourself to loving before being loved, Jesus will salvage a heart made sick by unrealized hopes. He is a King who satisfies.

The impact of one hope-filled encounter with Jesus set off a chain of events which overturned every indictment of despair and discouragement that came before. Jesus brings a hope that shakes things up. He restored the hope of the woman at the well and changed her life. However, it did not stop there. A confrontation He had with a woman at a well liberated the woman He met there and altered the destinies of many. An entire village came to know our Messiah because one woman was offered a drink of living water.

The rest of our chapter verse in Proverbs reads; "... but a longing fulfilled is a tree of life" (Proverbs 13:12b). A satisfied person feeds many people. One woman (whose name we do not know), sick with hopelessness, met Hope at a well and had her craving for worth fulfilled. She became a tree of life, impacting countless neighbors that day, and millions more in the centuries that followed.

I realize some of us have been shrouded in hopelessness for so long we know no other way of existing. Fear of disappointment immobilizes us, preventing us from reaching into our stepfamily relationships. It can be scary to step from behind the mask and place hope in God, especially when we do not know what it means to have hope fulfilled. Beloved, let me reiterate: God is faithful. He can be trusted with your expectations for better days. He satisfies us with Himself, so that we, like the woman at the well, can become hope filled, joy-full ambassadors of His grace in our families and everywhere we go.

May I pray with you?

I pray now, according to Romans 15:13, with confident expectation for answered prayer, that the God of hope will fill you with all joy and peace in believing, so that by the power of the Holy Spirit you may abound, bubble over and overflow in confident expectation that the goodness of God is available to you to bring about His good plans for you and for your family! In Jesus' Name. Amen!

TREASURE HUNT

Alright sisters, it's time to go on a little adventure. Grab your tools, namely your bible, journal, and pen, and let's do a little digging.

Take a doubt inventory in your life. What are the key points of doubt that have taken hold of your relationship with your stepchildren? Where is the doubting attitude evident in your interactions?

Read Psalm 48:14. How does knowing God will guide you until the end feed your hope?

What are the consequences of the doubts you experience? Focus on the emotional, physical and spiritual areas of your life. What scriptures will help you replace a doubting attitude with biblical hope?

CAN I GET OFF NOW?

I was a middle-aged runaway. I know that sounds like the beginning of a gas station novella, nevertheless, it's true. I ran away hard and fast one cold Michigan winter morning. At the ripe old age of 41. Years old. Not 5. Not 14. Not even 20. 41.

It was near Christmas. Jonathan and I had been married a little less than two years. At the time we maintained two residences so my daughter Kayla could finish high school in the community where she grew up. Our homes were 61 miles from each other, door to door. It worked for us because Jonathan travelled during the week and was home only on the weekends. I would stay in one home and check on the other during the week. We would alternate homes on weekends. The day I ran away we were at the home my husband brought into the marriage.

My stepchildren were with us this particular weekend and would stay a few extra days for Christmas break. It had been another one filled with sullen expressions, silent treatments, hot and cold reactions, and tension. Christmas had always been a special time for me and I worked very hard to make it special for everyone. It was important to me to make connections. However, no matter what I did, I could not break through to my stepchildren. That weekend I decided I was done riding the emotional rollercoaster. It was an especially difficult weekend because Kayla was at our other home with my Mom. I was away from my daughter, with kids who didn't necessarily want me to be with them, and it felt unfair of me to communicate my feelings to my husband. I was alone (or so I thought), isolated (or so I thought), mad (definitely), and tired (utterly). Just plain ole worn out. As I reread this paragraph it shames me to realize how often "I" was at the forefront in my thinking, but there it is.

Monday morning, I haughtily announced, "I need a break!" I packed my bag and prepared to make the 61-mile trek "home." Jonathan quietly said, "Okay, baby." I will never forget the hurt expression on his face. I can't even imagine the thoughts going through my husband's head as I drove away. I made it clear to him I had no intention of giving up on us; I just needed space, time, a haven. It must have cut him to the quick to hear I did not consider his home, now our home, emotionally safe for me that weekend.

The further I drove away from my husband and towards my "home" the worse I felt. Worse because I felt disconnected from this man to whom I had vowed my love, loyalty and fidelity. Worse because I felt I was at the end of a brittle rope which could snap at any moment, and I didn't want to cut anyone loose, nor did I wish to be cut loose. Worse because I absolutely knew I was not handling this in a way that honored my marriage, my husband, or God.

The further I drove away from my husband and towards my "home," the better I felt. Better because the further I drove the more my shoulders relaxed, and the lighter the air became. Better because I was going to see the one person who was a continuous source of joy in my life. Better because, for the moment, I was off the ride. The mixed-bag of emotions was driving me crazy.

BUILT FOR IT

My mother is afraid of heights. She's the type of afraid that will not drive over a bridge if she can help it. Somehow, her friends talked her into riding a rollercoaster at Cedar Point in Sandusky, Ohio. Home of the most rollercoasters in the world. Why she was even at the park I will never know, but there she sat, strapped into the seat, hands glued to the lap bar with the Vulcan death grip. The bell rang, and the coaster began its slow ascent up the lift hill. *Click-clack. Click-clack. Click-clack.* By the tenth clack, my mom was on the edge of madness. She turned into She-Hulk. Before her friends knew they had a disaster in the making, she shimmied out of the seat and was climbing out of the coaster as it was climbing up the hill. Thankfully, one of her friends was able to restrain her. What my mother experienced on a physical rollercoaster years ago, I experienced on an emotional rollercoaster the weekend I ran away. As the sensation of peril, real or imagined, set in, anxiety heightened, panic approached, and, like my mother, I determined one thing, "Get off...now!!!"

Am I the only one who rides an emotional rollercoaster in this blended family life? Happy one minute, sad the next? Hopeful as you set out on a family outing in the morning, deeply disappointed at night because moodiness, and misunderstanding, obliterated your expectations? Excited because, you've given love, and kindness, which could be reciprocated any moment, yet calloused at the apathetic responses from the people around you?

I discovered some very interesting facts while researching rollercoasters for this chapter. Did you know they were built for turbulence? The designers of a coaster know the ride will be thrilling but also dangerous. They are aware riders will get jerked around a bit. However, no matter how high, how fast, how many twists and turns, or drops and dips in the ride, the engineers design, create, and equip the coaster to withstand turbulence while keeping you safe.

It's the same for your stepmom ride. You were built for the excitement, joy, and turbulence of the life you're living. No matter how many ups and downs your heart experiences, God has equipped you to withstand the agitation, obey Him, and eventually find joy in everything, even loving your stepchildren without being loved in return. When Paul prayed for the believers at Colosse, he reminded them of God's glorious might at work in them to endure, withstand, and to do so with patience. The Young's Literal Translation of Colossians 1:9 – 11 reads as follows:

Because of this, we also, from the day in which we heard, do not cease praying for you, and asking that you may be filled with the full knowledge of His will in all wisdom and spiritual understanding, to your walking worthily of the Lord to all pleasing, in every good work being fruitful, and increasing to the knowledge of God, in all might being made mighty according to the power of His glory, to all endurance and long-suffering with joy.

You can hang on because you're not gripping with the power of your own strength. Our weaknesses are the perfect canvas upon which God paints His strength. It is His might which sees us through. It is His wisdom upon which we rely. It is His glory which enables us to hang in there. Through Him, we can overcome the difficult parts of every good work He has given us to accomplish, our "stepmomming" included. Actually, not only are we equipped to endure parenting-in-step, but the Bible tells us we need to endure and persevere so that after we have done God's will, we can receive His promise (Hebrews 10:36). God always has goodness in store for you and your family, but to experience the goodness you have to suffer the not so good.

Rollercoasters are marvels, engineered so that riders can maintain stability during a ride in which they indulge specifically for the thrill of its instability. The climb to dizzying heights followed by a rapid plunge into valleys keeps us on edge, and that's precisely why we ride. I am challenged to approach life in my stepfamily with the same degree of thrilled anticipation; knowing I will experience the peaks of joy and valleys of heartache, but not knowing when. Perhaps, our struggle with the unknown is purposeful. Some agitation is good for the soul.

GOOD VIBRATIONS

The Bible tells us in Hebrews 4:12:

For the word of God is living and active, sharper than any two-edged sword, piercing to the division of soul and of spirit, of joints and of marrow, and discerning the thoughts and intentions of the heart.

The Word of God causes disturbance and turbulence, it distinguishes between behavior reminiscent of the old carnal nature and behavior which conforms to the spirit. It alerts us to our motivations and intentions. It is like the leveler used to make sure the picture you're hanging is not crooked. Our eyes can trick us. We need an objective, true, and consistent measuring tool. To determine if our thinking is off or straight, we measure it against the sure, steady, word of God.

God will agitate us. He will slice us open. He does so with His word, and He allows it through circumstances.
Psalm 119:71 reads:

It is good for me that I have been afflicted; that I might learn Your statutes.

If we read earlier in Psalm 119, we will find the psalmist adrift. In verse 67 he writes:

Before I was afflicted I went astray, but now I keep Your word.

Ease allowed the psalmist to let up on his commitment to obey the Lord. Again, some agitation is good for the soul. The affliction the writer of this psalm went through brought his thinking back in alignment with God's truth. The unrest he experienced had an objective. It taught him a lesson. A difficult lesson. Those are the best kind. Difficult to obtain, difficult to forget. Perhaps the agitation we experience in the ups and downs of stepfamily life are purposeful; used by God to expose some area in our thinking which needs realignment. Maybe, rather than trying to escape the ride, we should ask God what He wants to call to our attention.

Lean in, my friend. Press into the turbulence. The agitation. See what it uncovers. Agitation reveals what dominates our hearts; whether fear, pride, and control, or faith, humility, and trust. Agitation provides an opportunity for us to seek God. Sometimes, the Lord allows agitation so that we will seek Him. Agitation may be problematic but it isn't always a problem.

JUST THE TIP OF THE ICEBERG

Don't you love how natural law demonstrates spiritual principles? God's attributes are on display in the diversity of snowflakes, the artistry of changing leaves in autumn, the purity of a baby's belly laugh, the physics behind a rollercoaster ride.

For instance, rollercoasters do not have a motor or an engine. They do not complete the ride under their own power. Coasters are "launched" into their rides by one of several different kinds of launches used to maximize speed and accuracy. A well-designed roller coaster will run through the entire ride on a single launch using its energy and momentum. They are designed to operate based on the laws of gravity, and kinetic and potential energy. Natural principles which have impact on objects regardless of the objects' characteristics. Biblical principles operate simply because God is sovereign. Applying Godly wisdom and principles to our stepparenting, and understanding the deeper work is accomplished by His Spirit alone, keeps our momentum going towards His desired end.

Many components create the supporting structure and the track system of rollercoasters, however, whether the coaster is made of wood, steel, or some composite material, steel is always used at critical joints. Steel is used to fortify the coaster at stress points, places where continued pressure is likely to cause a breech in proper operation. No matter what structure your blended family takes, the complexities, or the lack thereof, there are inherent dynamics which will stress your family in specific areas.

The Bible tells us in Psalm 9:9 "The Lord also will be a stronghold for the oppressed, a stronghold in times of trouble..." You will arrive at critical junctures in your stepfamily ride but remember God fortifies you in times of trouble.

Steel coasters provide a smooth ride, but wooden structures are designed to move under the force of passing cars. They wobble but the shaking and swaying motion is a deliberate design feature; to absorb the impact of the train. Flexibility is imperative. Paul wrote to the Philippians in the 12th and 13th verses of chapter 4:

> "I know both how to have a little, and I know how to have a
> lot. In any and all circumstances I have learned the secret of
> being content – whether well fed or hungry, whether in
> abundance or in need. I am able to do all things through Him
> who strengthens me." (HCSB)

The secret to Paul's ability to remain emotionally stable and satisfied, whether up or down, rich or poor, welcomed or rebuffed, was relying on the strength of Christ to see Him through whatever circumstances he faced. Our resilience and ability to remain pliable as we navigate stepfamily life lies in relying on Christ.

A roller coaster is attached to the tracks by double wheels. One set of wheels is on top of the track and the other is under the track. That two-pronged safety measure keeps the cars from falling off. The Word of God declares in 2 Thessalonians 3:3:

> "But the Lord is faithful, and He will strengthen you and
> protect you from the evil one."

Jesus is committed to your success in what He has called you to do. He bookends your stepmomming with strength and protection to keep you safe on the ride.

A rollercoaster's ride comes to a stop when the brake system is deployed. The brake system is on the track and not on the coaster. Brakes are at the end of the ride and situated along the track for emergency stops. We have no control, but we don't have to worry. If something untoward occurred during the ride, the brakes would engage to stop the ride. Provisions are made to prevent disaster. The Bible encourages us in Proverbs 3:25-26, "Have no fear of sudden disaster or of the ruin that overtakes the wicked, for the Lord will be your confidence and will keep your feet from being snared." Let me tell you something my sisters, God has your back! Stepparent in faith. We don't have control, but neither should we worry. God has made provision to prevent sudden disaster or ruin. Have confidence in His faithfulness and look to Him for the wisdom to stay out of the traps the enemy has set for you and your family.

HANGING ON

A rollercoaster-ride is over in three minutes...max. When we get on, we know there's a fixed point in time in which the ride will end. When the ride is over, we experience relief, exhilaration, even giddiness. I usually exit the ride saying how much fun I had and debating whether or not we should ride again. My husband exits the ride stating he's never getting on again. My mother has never ridden a rollercoaster since that first attempt over 40 years ago.

We can't say the same with riding an emotional rollercoaster. Often, we didn't choose to get on that ride. Suddenly, we're riding; being jerked around, flipped upside down, click-clacking our way to ridiculous heights only to come plummeting to the ground moments later. Ride it long enough and you will find yourself in the depths of despair which leaves you wanting nothing more than to get off.

Yet, it is into this despair, God sends His grace to relieve the heart-nausea which makes us want to cut and run. As we are learning to hang on, there are ways in which we can cooperate with the work of grace in our lives to maintain a balanced sense of well-being, peace, and hope while we experience the ups and downs:

◊ Make no rash decisions. Think twice before acting. When our hearts are famished or sick, our erratic emotions can lead to irrational actions. Take a few breaths to calm down before responding to someone; defer decision making until you've taken time to pray and talk through your feelings.

◊ Spend time with friends or in activities that feed your soul. Feeding your soul is an oft-overlooked enterprise which pays off in immediate delight. I like photography. I am in no way good at it but I get excited just thinking about grabbing my camera, a few lenses, and getting into the sunshine. When I find myself dealing with a little too much blended family madness, I grab my gear and head out for a few hours of shooting. It engages my mind and heart in an activity which brings me joy and helps bring equilibrium to my life.

◊ Trust God to provide a well-spring in the desert. God does not always immediately deliver us from the cracked, dry places in our families, but He will cause a river to spring up unexpectedly. Look for the flow.

◊ Rehearse your God stories. When Israel, David, and others in the Bible, needed encouragement, they remembered and recounted the goodness, faithfulness, promises, and miraculous acts of God. Recalling that God moved on your behalf in the past assures your heart of help in the future so that you "ride in hope" when life throws you for a loop.

◊ But don't ignore the struggles you've been facing. Use a journal to get them off your chest, clarify your thoughts, and pray for restored hope and peace.

◊ Forgive your family members for the words and actions which sent you hurtling towards the ground at top speed.

◊ Harness the negative thoughts that make you want to quit and replace them with God's truth. Sit with the feelings these thoughts engender, work through them. They are real. Nevertheless, remind yourself that God's truth is more real than any lie being spoken to you through the filter of hurt feelings.

◊ Don't ride alone. Invite someone to journey with you. We lose perspective when we're isolated. Share your desire for stability in your family with other people like your spouse, mentor, or trusted friend, and ask them to pray with and for you.

Near tragedy drew me back home that fateful weekend. When I left, my husband and I had been removing wallpaper from the dining room walls. He kept working after I left. As he scraped, his hand slipped and he sliced open a finger, nearly detaching it. No one was there to take him to the hospital. I raced "home." All of my sour feelings evaporated the moment I heard he was hurt and essentially alone.

I am so glad I did not stay away. I am grateful we stuck it out and experienced the adventures, trips, laughter, and growth. I returned to celebration in good times, comfort in hard times, the pleasure of raising a son, and the fun of multiple daughters laughing around the table. I returned so my daughter could know the strength of a caring father and Jonathan and I could have an extraordinary relationship.

The short answer to, "Can I get off now?" is, no! Not if you want more than temporary relief. You were made to persevere through the emotional turbulence of living in step. Keep loving. Keep believing. Keep hoping. God knows you are a mom with children not biologically your own. Girl, you need Jesus! The Lord is with you. Holding your hand. Now strap in for the ride of your life.

TREASURE HUNT

Alright sisters, it's time to go on a little adventure. Grab your tools, namely your bible, journal, and pen, and let's do a little digging.

What is agitating you about your interactions with your bonus children? How might God be using that to grow you into more Christlikeness?

Reread the list of ways in which we can cooperate with the work of God's grace to maintain stability on this rollercoaster of a ride we call living in-step.

    ◊   Which two actions are you going to take?
    ◊   Why did you choose those specific actions?
    ◊   How will incorporating these actions serve you as a stepmom?

Now spend some time in prayer, asking God to help you remain emotionally steady in your family, to anchor you in His word, and to help you as you lean on His strength to embody the actions you're taking.

PRUNE YOUR HEART

Loving while waiting to be loved consists of fearlessness, patience, hope, and stability, intertwined like an intricate bow on a gift. If you pull away one, the whole thing comes apart. Without fearlessness, waiting intimidates us. Without patience, waiting becomes unbearable. Without hope, waiting defeats us. Without stability, waiting disarms us. The Word of God helps us stash a haul of bravery, patience, hope, and stability upon which we can draw.

When tempted by Satan in the wilderness, Jesus overcame the wicked one with the Word of God. Each attempt by the enemy to lead the Holy One astray was met with the Sword of Truth. In inspiring the writers of the gospels to include this encounter (Matthew 4:1-11, Mark 1:12-13, and Luke 4:1-13), God did more than record a pre-ministry event in the life of our Savior. Jesus is our model for defeating the lies of the enemy in our lives today, a strategy spelled out in James 4:7:

Submit yourselves to God. Resist the devil, and he will flee from you.

My sweet sister, you are in a battle. There's a war raging over your precious identity as an heir of God, joint heir with Jesus Christ, and all that's attached to your "new man" status. The enemy uses lies, born out of emotional wounds, to keep us from the truth: redeemed is both your story and your status. The enemy knows his lies would lose their grip if you could not only believe but accept you are the object of God's affection and love; His ransomed daughter made righteous and holy by the righteousness of Christ. God desires for each of us to experience the freedom of living whole.

It is time to rid your heart of anything which threatens to blind you to truth. It is time to surrender to God's truth. Pray, rehearse, and meditate on, God's word until it is soaked into the fabric of your being. His Word is living, it is powerful, it divides soul from spirit, it slices through lies, and fuels Holy Spirit empowered living and loving. When the enemy returns to tempt us again, we resist him with continued truth. God's word promises the enemy will flee from us.

I have listed just a few of the 100's of scriptures listed in the Bible which speaks of our identity in Christ. Please take a moment to look over these scriptures. Pray over them. Memorize them and hide them in your heart. Ask questions of them. Ask God to open your understanding as you read. Most importantly, believe them and ask the Holy Spirit to help any unbelief.

I praise you because I am fearfully and wonderfully made; your works are wonderful, I know that full well. Psalm 139:14

Before I formed you in the womb, I knew you, before you were born, I set you apart; I appointed you as a prophet to the nations.
Jeremiah 1:5

Yet to all who did receive him, to those who believed in his name, he gave the right to become children of God. John 1:12

I no longer call you servants, because a servant does not know his master's business. Instead, I have called you friends, for everything that I learned from my Father I have made known to you. John 15:15

You did not choose me, but I chose you and appointed you so that you might go and bear fruit—fruit that will last—and so that whatever you ask in my name the Father will give you.
John 15:16

For we know that our old self was crucified with him so that the body ruled by sin might be done away with, that we should no longer be slaves to sin. Romans 6:6

Therefore, there is now no condemnation for those who are in Christ Jesus. Romans 8:1

No, in all these things we are more than conquerors through him who loved us. Romans 8:37

For I am convinced that neither death nor life, neither angels nor demons, neither the present nor the future, nor any powers, neither height nor depth, nor anything else in all creation, will be able to separate us from the love of God that is in Christ Jesus our Lord. Romans 8:38-39

But whoever is united with the Lord is one with him in spirit. 1 Corinthians 6:17

Therefore, if anyone is in Christ, he is a new creation; old things have passed away; behold, all things have become new. 2 Corinthians 5:17

So in Christ Jesus you are all children of God through faith, Galatians 3:26

Praise be to the God and Father of our Lord Jesus Christ, who has blessed us in the heavenly realms with every spiritual blessing in Christ. Ephesians 1:3

*In him we have redemption through his blood, the forgiveness
of sins, in accordance with the riches of God's grace.
Ephesians 1:7*

*And God raised us up with Christ and seated us with him in
the heavenly realms in Christ Jesus. Ephesians 2:6*

*For we are God's handiwork, created in Christ Jesus to do
good works, which God prepared in advance for us to do.
Ephesians 2:10*

*But now in Christ Jesus you who once were far away have
been brought near by the blood of Christ. Ephesians 2:13*

*But our citizenship is in heaven. And we eagerly await a
Savior from there, the Lord Jesus Christ. Philippians 3:20*

*Since, then, you have been raised with Christ, set your hearts
on things above, where Christ is, seated at the right hand of
God. Set your minds on things above, not on earthly things.
For you died, and your life is now hidden with Christ in God.
When Christ, who is your life, appears, then you also will
appear with him in glory.
Colossians 3:1-4*

*But you are a chosen people, a royal priesthood, a holy nation,
God's special possession, that you may declare the praises of
him who called you out of darkness into his wonderful light. 1
Peter 2:9*

SECTION II

The Focused Heart

Lord, fill me with more of You!

MEASURED MOMS

I think I have become pretty skilled at schooling my expressions. I try very hard not to telegraph my thoughts through my reactions. It is a critical tool used in making people feel safe enough to express everything in their hearts. Years of practice have helped me hone skills at maintaining a neutral posture and expression in conversation. Still, I nearly lost it in a conversation with one of my bonus children:

"Your consistent love made all the difference, Cheryl. You have given me hope that I can have my own family and that it will work."

WHAT'S YOUR WHY?

We are not often gifted with a "Well Done" on this side of the Judgement Seat of Christ. We do what we do because we love God and desire to please Him. To hear His pleasure echoed through my bonus daughter's words were my near undoing. She has no idea how many times I wanted to give up and stop trying. She has no idea how many times I cried out to God for strength and help; how many times I felt defeated. How many times the enemy of my soul whispered words which fed discouragement and inadequacy. The nights I breathlessly prayed, "God, I can't", to which He'd inevitably assure me with, "I know, but I can." However, Papa knew my struggle. He chose unexpected words in an inconsequential moment to encourage me to keep doing what is good.

Consistency is exhausting. I am not nearly as jazzed to work out on Day 20 as I was on Day 1. Of course, I know without Day 20 I will never reach the goals of lowering my A1C, better quality of life in my old age, mental acuity, and fitting into my size 8 jeans again. So, I trudge through Day 20, resenting its necessity. Consequently, I'm not as motivated on Day 21. By day 28, I'm over it. The struggle is real. The only thing that keeps me going are the eventual payoffs: the achievement of goals, the look my husband gets on his face when he watches me walk away, higher brain function, and more energy.

If the desire for the payoff is severe enough, it will carry me through the inevitable collapse of my motivation. For Stepmoms, the payoff to loving while we wait to be loved is far more substantial than looking cute in our clothes.

Our "why" will energize us. Our "why" will prop up tenacity. Methods, strategies, and blueprints give us a roadmap but without a compelling "why," our "want to" will fizzle out. God wants more than invitation into our struggles. He wants more than robotic obedience. God wants a deep surrender to Him in our step-mothering so that we reflect His steady love and overwhelming goodness to our families. He wants a relationship. One that includes heart to heart encounters with Him, in which we fall to our knees in worship, and rise in love-sick, awe-struck obedience. Glorifying Him in all I do has become my "why".

WHAT CHA' LOOKING FOR?

God commands attentiveness in how we conduct our lives. Intentionality matters. Defined intentions are reached intentions. Prudent choices matter. Well thought out strategies, based on biblical truth, make a difference. Paul admonished Timothy to hold on to the pattern of sound teaching that he heard from Paul; to lean on the Holy Spirit to help him guard the deposit entrusted to him (2 Timothy 1:13-14). We do not exchange a list of "to don'ts" for a list of "to dos". If that happened, we would get lost in performance. Performance keeps us locked on outcomes. There is no life in performance. No abundance in performance. Better decisions, better living, and better loving spring from intentions deposited and purified by the Holy Spirit; and purified intentions spring from a ransomed, focused heart in love with the King.

Eternal life is found in knowing God and the One He sent, Jesus Christ. You and I have been chosen to know Him and experience His love. In response, we follow His greatest command, to love Him first and best. His love then empowers us to follow His second greatest command, that we love others. Moms with focused hearts redirect their attention from the outcomes of their efforts. For them, loving their bonus children is an act of honor and obedience to God. The great blessing for those who persist in obedience is pleasing the Love of their life. The outcomes of our obedience belong to Him. Resolute stepmoms, determined to love before being loved, quickly learn that the reactions of their stepchildren are a faulty measurement of progress. Stepchildren are of two minds when interacting with stepmoms. They like us today, feel guilty for that, then compensate by being distant, or outright mean. The litmus test for success as a stepmom is that mom's response to God's direction. The resolute bonus mom is steadfast, unmovable, unshakable, always excelling; doing more than just enough, in the service of the Lord (1 Corinthians 15:58). Regardless of what her children do, she knows her labor in the service of the Lord is not in vain.

In this section of Waiting to be Wanted we are going to chat about four key characteristics displayed in the heart of a focused Stepmom: convinced, flexible, strategic, and merciful. A chapter is devoted to each characteristic. This section ends with, "Plant Your Heart", a chapter filled with "if/then" promises from scripture to encourage stepmoms to cooperate with the work of the Holy Spirit in their hearts.

Friend, let me tell you, "Jesus, help me love this child like You love me," is a dangerous prayer! When we resolve to be like Jesus then opportunities to be like Jesus will show up. Ready. Set. Go.

SPARKED

Jeremiah sat with his hands crossed over his chest. Everything about his posture indicated he was not interested in what was being said. He was present but not involved. His contribution to the counseling session was thirty minutes of stubborn silence. The counselor tried again with a direct question.

"Jeremiah, do you want your marriage?"

Jeremiah exploded, "We don't have a marriage! I have tried. My children have tried. Heck, even my ex has tried to reach out to Susan for the sake of the kids. She constantly rejects us. She doesn't know how to love us. She doesn't even try to pretend. I don't know what happened. I'm tired. Sex is no good. I'm not the one you should be asking if this marriage is wanted. I cannot do this another day. I want a wife, not this!"

Susan shrank in her chair, tears running down cheeks. The counselor swiveled in her chair to face Susan. "Susan, I think it may be time to tell Jeremiah about some of the challenges you've been having." Susan sat without blinking, lost in her thoughts. She tried to conjure up enough courage to open up so perhaps she can have the marriage she dreamed of when she married Jerry and became stepmom to his three children. He was right. Everyone tried. Everyone but her. She didn't know what to do. She could feel the anxiety mounting. "Why is this happening," she thought. "Why can't I just love people? What's wrong with me? Why is everything a battle?" Her breathing quickened. She was on the verge of a panic attack. "It's now or never, Susan," she silently scolded. She worked her mouth but the words were trapped. They would not climb over the knot in her throat. She chanced a look at her husband of five years.

Jerry had tears in his eyes! "Please, Suze," he begged, "Please."

Susan closed her eyes, took a deep breath, opened her mouth, and forced out the words. "My father ..."

CIVIL WAR

The ambition of my heart as a daughter of God can be summed up by a prayer Paul prayed for the Ephesians:

> I pray that out of his glorious riches He may strengthen you with power through His Spirit in your inner being, so that Christ may dwell in your hearts through faith. And I pray that you, being rooted and established in love, may have power, together with all the Lord's holy people, to grasp how wide and long and high and deep is the love of Christ, and to know this love that surpasses knowledge—that you may be filled to the measure of all the fullness of God.

Ephesians 3:16-19

My greatest desire is to know and experience Jesus, be entrenched in His love as the ambient thread of my life and be filled with the fullness of God. As we enjoy the wonders of His love, we become intimate with the acceptance, security, confidence, and friendship found there, which liberate us to love unreservedly.

When I hear a stepmom say she's unable to love her stepchild, I know I am listening to a woman at war with herself. This is a woman who has not yet begun to grasp the depth of love God has for her, or for the children in her care. Perhaps, there are mitigating factors at play. Elements of her life, her past, or her journey which prevent her from experiencing or giving love. At the heart of my, and Susan's, inability to freely give and receive love was rejection.

"I don't want to go to the bathroom with her!" The class erupted in laughter. She was the new girl in class and already very popular. I was the unpopular, quiet girl who had few friends. Those who reached out to me in friendship were afraid to come to my defense when the popular kids decided to single me out. Which was often. The teacher chose me to escort the new girl to the bathroom because I was the only who had completed my work. My only consolation was the look of regret on the girl's face. She apologized as we walked to the bathroom. Eventually she and I became friends, but I never forgot the shame of being the object of classroom ridicule. Or my 5th grade teacher, Mrs. Schmansky. I was so dejected, after that incident, I wrote a letter stating I wanted to kill myself. My teacher called my mother for a parent-teacher's conference. She spoke words in that conference which brought a bit of solace. I thank God for the wisdom He gave my teacher, but the rejection stung, and stuck.

Both Susan and I suffered from emotional injuries. She, from her father, mine from peers. Whenever we faced subsequent injuries, as is prone to happen in this broken world, the lies which lodged in our hearts from those initial injuries became more deeply embedded. Why is it easy to believe people who act carelessly with our hearts and so hard to believe God? Perhaps you have an emotional injury for which there has been no redress, nothing acknowledged, repented for, or repaid to you. Perhaps you're still dealing with the by-product. An ignored injury makes it seem as if you're going through life unavenged, unanswered and unhealed. It creates an emotional void which makes it difficult to give love. To that, we pile on guilt for being stingy with love, yet feel helpless to do anything about it. If this is you, it's going to be okay. Freedom and wholeness await you.

SCARRED LOVE

When we think of the love of God, we typically go to the New Testament, to Golgotha. His love is on visceral display on the cross. We don't think of the smiting God in the Old Testament as primarily loving. He is holy, sovereign, defending, yes. Loving? We're not too sure. Yet, it is in the Old Testament we find a song celebrating His great love (Psalm 136). The writer begins the song with a proclamation: *Give thanks to the Lord, for He is good, His faithful love endures forever.* We have reason to awake every morning with a yelled out loud, "God, I thank you!" The Lord is good, the Lord is loving, and His intentional good towards us never stops.

The psalmist follows that opening with examples of God's mighty acts, beginning with acts of creation, then celebrating acts which directly helped Israel. The congregation responds each and every time with, "His love endures forever;" a reminder that God's love is eternal, everlasting, unending. His love was on display before the cross. His love is displayed on the cross. His love is displayed today.

We are enabled to love without being loved as we remain aware of God's goodness and faithfulness. We will only recognize and receive God's goodness and faithfulness when we're convinced of God's love. The best way to be convinced of His love today is to remember, rehearse, and celebrate His past goodness. Let's take a moment to write our own Goodness Psalm. I will use my name and some of my experiences as an example:

> *Rejoice, Cheryl! Give thanks to God, for He is good and His love endures forever! He has done great wonders. His love goes on forever He set the stars in the heavens His love endures forever He walked through the brokenness of my life and restored me His love endures forever He healed and redeemed me His love endures forever He blessed me with a daughter out of a barren womb His love endures forever! He sent comfort when I was discouraged His love endures forever He set me in a place of refreshing His love endures forever!*

Your turn! Go ahead, remind yourself. Revisit His intervention and rescue. Recall the presence of His love in moments when you felt devastated and in moments of rejoicing. In this Psalm, and the song we each will write, we recall that God's love is expansive and individual. It is general and unique. It is broad and targeted.

His love is exhibited in vivid splendor in the scarred hands of our Risen King. Wounded by your sin. Pierced by mine. Crucified for our crimes against God, He loves us. When He could have called for rescue, His love for the Father and His love for us kept Him lifted on Skull Hill, suspended between Heaven and Earth. His resurrection did not rob Him of the memory. Our victorious, resurrected King wears the scars of loving, His badges of honor, in His hands and side. When Thomas doubted the news of Jesus' resurrection, Jesus appeared, and invited Thomas to examine the wounds; to touch and handle the evidence of His adoration and victory (John 20:24-29). Today, He is inviting you to examine, investigate, and be convinced of His reality and love.

I lack the skill to take you on an expedition into the depths of God's love worthy of the subject. We will spend eternity exploring and enjoying the treasure of it. I will simply quote the disciple whom Jesus loves, John. He writes in the third chapter of his first letter:

This is how we have come to know love: He laid down His life for us. We should also lay down our lives for our brothers and sisters. 1 John 3:16

He then writes in 1 John 4:7-11:

Dear friends, let us love one another, for love comes from God. Everyone who loves has been born of God and knows God. Whoever does not love does not know God, because God is love. This is how God showed his love among us: He sent his one and only Son into the world that we might live through him. This is love: not that we loved God, but that he loved us and sent his Son as an atoning sacrifice for our sins. Dear friends, since God so loved us, we also ought to love one another.

Love is demonstrated in how God loves us. First. Sacrificially. Unreservedly. Sweet lady, that scripture is talking about you! You are the focus of God's love. You are the disciple whom God loves. Say that to yourself, *"I am the one whom God loves!"* His life was laid down for you. He fought for you. He is here for you. You and I are acquainted with Love. Despite Susan's father, despite my childhood friends, despite what has happened in your life. Right now, you know Love and He knows you. You are the one called by Him to demonstrate His love; first, sacrificially, unreservedly.

A stepmom with an anemic view of God's love has no hope for that love to help her break through what holds her captive. No hope for demonstrating His love to others. However, for the stepmom willing to take God at His word, she quickly realizes God's love isn't passive. He isn't only patient, kind, and gentle. His love is that of a fierce warrior. His love roars like a conquering King. His love is powerful. His love is power. Supernatural. His love destroys sin. It is a deathblow to death. Delivers from the grave. His love chases away fear. Sets free. Transforms. His love is mighty, and nothing, not even death, can pry us from its grip.

It is into this love we have been reborn. We are daughters of a Father who is love, therefore, we know love, and can share our Father's love.

LIKE FATHER, LIKE DAUGHTER

I have been told I look just like my father, with hair. My father and his sisters favor each other as well, one sister in particular. As my grandmother tells the story, I was at her house one day when my aunt's date arrived to pick her up for an outing. I came toddling into the living room and the guy stared at me. He turned to my aunt, turned to me, turned back to my aunt, then looked at my grandmother who had been silently watching him. She smiled and said, "That's not her baby. That's her brother's child." He laughed, rubbed his knees, and smiled, exclaiming, "Whew!"

I look like my father. I'm also told from time to time I act like my mother. We take on the physical and behavioral attributes of our natural parents and family by way of genetics and proximity. Hearing I look or act like my family affirms a sense of belonging.

You and I are partakers of God's divine nature (2 Peter 1:4). The characteristics of God's nature become our own through the transforming power of the Holy Spirit at work in us. They become more prominent as we spend time in proximity to our Father and our brothers and sisters in Christ. I want that. Yearn for it. Hearing we look and act like our Father affirms our sense of belonging. Which is why living with anything less launches us into civil war.

Laurie's face told the tale her words could not express. Sullen expression, downturned lips, defiant eyes, clenched fists, and tense shoulders clearly communicated her "I'm over it" attitude.

"Look, I don't care if she does live with us, as far as I'm concerned, she doesn't count! My marriage comes first and I'm tired of her interference in our lives. I'm not bending over backwards for her anymore. She's going to be gone in a couple years anyway so I just need to hang on until then. I can't stand her. And, I don't want to love her!"

Laurie went on and on; the women around her grew quiet. Eventually she realized she had lost her "amen" corner. One brave friend, a true sister, reached across the table, cleared her throat, and spoke into the weighty silence:

"Laurie. Your heart is so ugly right now, but God wants to set you free. He wants to use you to reach your stepdaughter but you're so in love with yourself and your needs and your hurts, you can't see beyond you. His desire is for us to be like Him in the way He loves. That's what Jesus commanded, that we would love others in the same way He loves us. This is how He loves us, Laurie. While

---

we were His enemies, He died for you, for me, for your stepdaughter. Jesus didn't wait for us to act a certain way, to love Him, or even like Him. He loved us because that's who He is. And that's the kind of love He has placed in our hearts through His precious Holy Spirit. Love that will see your stepdaughter's pain, see her need, see her worth and respond because she's more important to you than you are. That's the love He will empower you to show your stepdaughter...the same kind He has shown to you."

Laurie's shoulders sagged and she burst into tears. The hardness in her heart bowed to the truth spoken with compassion, by a person whom I would say is her best friend. Laurie had a long way to go to reach consistency, but she took an important first step at the table.

The day I became a follower of Christ, I knelt in my dorm room and got up with a tangible sense of rightness, acceptance, and cleanliness on the inside; however, it wasn't long before I lost awareness of God's love in a real, "at this moment", experiential way. Life gets in the way and chokes out the intimacy of knowing. Intentionality and awareness are musts for keeping first things first.

Jesus tells us in Luke 21:34:

> "Be on guard, so that your hearts will not be weighted down with dissipation and drunkenness and the worries of life and that day will not come on you suddenly like a trap."

It thrills me that Jesus threw in "worries of life" as something against which we must guard. It may not be drunkenness, sexual immorality, or sins weighing us down, blinding us to intentionality, and living life in His purpose. Could it be that busyness is occupying our attention? Maybe it's dishes, bills, politics, children, good friends, stressful jobs, and bad marriages distracting us. Too much to do. Life!

The great thing about depletion is that it fosters desperation. One day I prayed, "Jesus, I want to love You more and love like You love. Please show me how." His answer was not what I expected.

FIRST LOVED

I stared in wonder at the nursing baby in my arms. After years of praying and believing God, we finally had a child of our own. Here was the one person in the entire universe for whom I knew I would sacrifice anything but my relationship with Christ. For this little one, no more than 30 days in the Earth, I would forgo wants, forgo needs, even die. As I memorized every strand of silky black hair on her head, and offered my finger as a squeeze toy for her tiny hand, I was arrested by a question bubbling in my heart, "Do you see how much you love her?"

The question startled me. Not because the Holy Spirit asked an unexpected question at an unexpected moment. I was stunned at the tenderness of the tone. The Father stepped into my new mom bubble as I sat completely in love with my daughter. It was a holy disruption meant to immerse my heart in the richness of I AM. I neither acknowledged nor answered the question. It was not time for responding. It was a holy moment, a time for silence. My living room became hallowed ground. Then the Spirit of the Lord impressed these words upon my heart, "I love you that much and more!"

My breath caught and the world exploded in a kaleidoscopic consequence of joy. I was a believing Christian, actively working in my home church, who prayed with others, and talked openly about my faith, but the tangible reality of God's love for me had faded. It was something I knew in my head and believed in my heart, yet it had been far too long since I related to His love within the context of daily life. He used the example of a mother's overwhelming love for her newborn to burn His indelible love on my soul. I understood immediately.

My newborn laid in arms, unaware of my love for her. She could do nothing for me. She simply existed; taking everything I offered, as if it were her right to do so. I freely, generously, and gladly gave her everything I knew to give. I loved her, not because she earned it, or reciprocated. I loved her then, and love her now, because I am her mother, and she is my daughter. Nothing will ever change that. That is what the Father communicated about His love for me.

What I had tried to accomplish through activity, study, and emotional stirring, was supernaturally imparted to me by the Spirit of the living God. He loved me; more than I loved the daughter in my arms. I am the disciple whom God loves. Elected. Wanted. Adored. His Son died for me some 2000 years ago, and He loved me deeply, passionately, actively, uniquely in that moment. In all my moments. I delight His heart. I bring Him joy. My bumbling efforts to grow up bring a smile to His face. He is my Father, and I am His daughter. I cannot disappoint Him for He is unaware of nothing. He knows everything I think, say, or do before it's thought, said, or done. I can do nothing to lose His love for I did nothing to gain His love. I am loved. Period.

Isn't that like our Father? To answer my question by revealing Himself? Almost as if He were saying, "You want to know how to love? Here...I AM!" He is love and to know Him is to be loved. In no more than a five-minute occurrence, initiated by the God who delivers us to Himself, I was drenched in love. That moment sparked a blaze which burns brighter day by day. That spark ignites peace and composure, submission and courage, hope and patience, freedom and wisdom. The more rooted I am in the truth that I am loved, secure, accepted, valued, for no other reason than He has claimed me as His own, the more I am able to love. It took time to grow into this greater awareness of His love. God used circumstances to break me free of old habits of mindless relating, but something ignited in my heart that day on the couch.

My friend, if you think this is a position exclusive to certain people, you are mistaken. You, too, are a woman well-loved by our Sovereign God. Therefore, you, too, are a woman who can love.

IT'S IN YOU

The faith of a focused stepmom is authentic. She lives what she believes. She knows the One she serves is real, His word is the standard, and His ways, although sometimes inscrutable, are, at all times, best. She is empowered to show His love consistently. She demonstrates to others what has been demonstrated to her. She is sparked.

I am old enough to have made popcorn the old-fashioned way; by heating up oil in a saucepan, pouring in the kernels once the oil is heated to the right temperature, and moving the pan back and forth over the fire until most of the kernels have popped. Never did all of the kernels pop. In order to enjoy a cup of popcorn you needed at least 10 minutes, and elbow grease. Eventually we got Jiffy Pop™. Then someone invented microwave popcorn.

Today, we simply stick a bag of popcorn in the microwave, set the timer, push "Start," then wait 3 minutes for a salty snack. Not a lot of effort on our part, but there's a whole lot going on in the popcorn bag.

A microwave pops the popcorn in a bag by stirring up the moisture inside the kernels. The bag keeps all of the steam and moisture trapped, allowing the kernels to heat up faster than they could on a stove top. Nothing is added beyond the spark of heat. Nothing else is needed. The moisture which causes the popcorn kernel to pop when sparked is already in the kernel. Let me write that again so you can read it again: the moisture, which causes the popcorn kernel to pop when sparked by the heat of the microwave, is already in the kernel.

Apostle Paul reminds us we too have been moisturized:

> Therefore, since we have been justified by faith, we have peace with God through our Lord Jesus Christ. Through him we have also obtained access by faith into this grace in which we stand, and we rejoice in hope of the glory of God. Not only that, but we rejoice in our sufferings, knowing that suffering produces endurance, and endurance produces character, and character produces hope, and hope does not put us to shame, because God's love has been poured into our hearts through the Holy Spirit who has been given to us.
> Romans 5:1-5 (ESV)

The Living Bible paraphrases Romans 5:5 as such:

> Then, when that happens, we are able to hold our heads high no matter what happens and know that all is well, for we know how dearly God loves us, and we feel this warm love everywhere within us because God has given us the Holy Spirit to fill our hearts with his love.

Oh, the time we've wasted searching for what God has already given.

Being justified by faith through our Lord Jesus Christ, we become the beneficiaries of a considerable inheritance in Christ. Salvation is ours through Him. Freedom is ours through Him. Peace, righteousness, joy, and reconciliation with God belongs to you and me. We stand in and have eternal access to magnificent grace. Rejoice in your hope in God. Rejoice in sufferings, too, because they produce endurance, character, and more hope. Our hope in God will not disappoint, delude, shortchange, or shame us, no matter what we face. We are absolutely convinced of God's goodness because the knowledge of and acquaintance with His astounding love for us is poured in our hearts by the Holy Spirit, who has also been given to us.

What a place of privilege! This intimate knowledge and experience of God's love, gifted to us by the Holy Spirit in our hearts, is more than security and heritage for us. It is the moisture which, when heated by the Holy Spirit, transforms us. God's love for us, received by faith, sets us free. His love, poured to overflowing, molds us into daughters who are held captive by His love and, therefore, can return His love and give His love to others by the power of His Holy Spirit.

According to Romans 5:5, the love we have in our hearts, given to us, then given back to God and given away to others, is the Greek word agape. Of the four types of love in the Bible, agape is the highest. Agape is the term used for God's love specifically. It defines an immeasurable, self-sacrificing, unconditional, incomparable love.

PASS IT ON

I had no intention of remarrying after my divorce. The years following the divorce was the first time in my adult life I was single, and I enjoyed them, immensely. God, however, had different plans.

About two years into my single lady season, I was driving down the street when the Spirit of the Lord impressed a question upon my heart, "If I were to bless you with a husband, what would you want?" Huh?! I verbally responded with something along the lines of, "I don't need a husband. I have You!" After which I "heard" in my heart, "I may bless you with a husband, but no one will ever love you like I love you!" A few months later Jonathan came back into my life; and he returned with the revelation of God's love for me burning in his heart.

One day Jonathan and I were bantering back and forth about who loved whom the most. Suddenly he became quite serious, touched my face, and said, "I know I love you more than you could love me.

"The love I have for you is an extension of your Father's love! It is Him loving you through me."

As much as I am loved by my husband, his love for me pales in comparison to God's love for me. As secure as I am as a wife, I am infinitely more secure as a daughter. Agape love is an indescribably selfless love completely committed to the good of others. Let me put is more accurately. Our indescribably selfless Heavenly Father is completely committed to your good! Moreover, He enables you and I to love others this same way. His love is poured into our hearts. Then, His Holy Spirit, causes us to be an extension of His love for others.

Agape love does not come from good intentions. It is born in the heart of our Savior, placed in our hearts by grace, and realized in our lives as a result of being filled with His Spirit.

You know what song is ringing in my soul right now? That old Sunday School song by Kurt Kaiser, "Pass It On". Let's read the first verse:

It only takes a spark to get a fire going
And soon all those around can warm up in its glowing.
That's how it is with God's love, once you've experienced it.
You spread His love to ev'ryone. You want to pass it on.

Did you sing it too? All it takes is one spark. One moment in which you become utterly convinced of the height, depth, breadth, and width of God's love for you. Like the moisture which is already inside a popcorn kernel, once agape, which is already in your heart, is sparked, it will expand in your life, blessing you and those around you.

Since you are deeply loved by God, you are not held to stereotypes and paradigms of competition, jealousy, and inadequacy commonly experienced within step relationships. Because you are loved by God, you can demonstrate, through your actions, what love does, regardless of the responses of others. As long as you remain in His love you can persevere, you can wait, because love, agape, endures all things (1 Corinthians 13:4-8). There is nothing agape won't brave for the good of others.

Go ahead. Pray that audacious prayer, "Jesus, I want to love like You love. Please show me how." Then ready your heart to be enraptured by God's focused, intentional, pursuing love for you.

TREASURE HUNT

Alright sisters, it's time to go on a little adventure. Grab your tools, namely your bible, journal, and pen, and let's do a little digging.

1 Corinthians 13:4-8 paints the picture of what agape looks like applied to everyday life. Take a moment to prayerfully read the scriptures. I encourage you to ready it in the Easy-to-Read Translation (ERV). As you read, note the times God has been patient with you, kind to you, took pleasure in your accomplishments, saw to your needs, etc.

Thank God for the tangible demonstration of His love.

How would you apply the characteristics of agape to your stepparenting?

THE (HE)ART OF RENEGOTIATION

I try to strike a balance in most areas of my life, but there are a few things which send me careening towards lopsided, heavy handedness; an all or nothing approach in the worst ways. Especially, when I, once again, decide it's time to get in shape.

"You can do it. Keep going."

Dr. Bernie was very encouraging on my first day of CrossFit. It was her testimony of beginning CrossFit when she was out of shape, losing weight, then becoming a trainer, which motivated my initial interest. With her success spurring me on, I thought I could do it too. I don't know what in the world I was thinking.

After 20 minutes of squats, jumps, and other stuff I can't even name, Dr. Bernie says,

"Okay, now let's get ready for your workout!"

My jaw dropped. Hadn't I already been working out?! Clearly, I was out of my depth!

CrossFit has a circuit workout consisting of three rounds of declining reps of exercises. The first round has 21 reps of about five "no sane person would do these" exercises. The second has 15 reps of those exercises. The last, 9. I made it through the first round. By the time I got to the butterfly sit-ups, the second exercise in the next round, I knew it was a wrap. For the uninformed, like me before attempting this insanity, butterfly sit-ups are full sit-ups with your knees bent, splayed out to the side, and the soles of your feet touching so that your legs form a wing shape. Who has time to think of this mess?! However, Dr. Bernie remained encouraging.

"Take your time."

"Okay, I'm going to try to do it but I don't think I'm going to make it past five."

"Just do as many as you can."

One. Barely. Two. I needed to close the "butterfly wings" for that one. Three. My abs shook and strained. My abs revolted on the fourth attempt, and my sit-up became a side-flop. I laughed as I laid on the floor. Message received: CrossFit was not for me. It was time for my body and my mind to renegotiate.

DETOURS

When Jonathan and I married, only Kayla, my bio-daughter, lived with us full-time. Our oldest, his stepdaughter from his first marriage, was in her early 20's. He never had any visitation order in place for her. There were court orders in place to manage visitation for his two bio children. They spent time with us two weekends out of the month. Summers and holidays were a bit more flexible. This was the schedule for the first three years of our marriage. All in all, a manageable routine.

In the course of 4 ½ years, my first marriage dissolved, we were divorced, he remarried a month later, I reconnected with Jonathan, my first husband died, and Jonathan and I were married. A lot of major change in a short period of time. After Jonathan and I married, we were able to create a schedule. I reluctantly adapted in the craziness of the previous years, so was overjoyed to have a dependable rhythm again. Finally, I could plan. Then came a fork in the road.

I enjoyed our life immensely. Not too much of my routine needed to change. Jonathan regularly traveled to the location of his out-of-town clients. He would fly out on Monday and return on Friday. I traveled with him a few times a year. Those were always fun excursions. Sometimes, if Jonathan was delayed returning home, I would pick up my bonus children for our time together.

About two years into our marriage, Jay, my stepson, began dropping hints about living with us. I didn't think much about it at the time. I would welcome him, of course, but I felt pretty certain this was not a bridge we would have to cross any time soon. Once, when he brought it up, my husband said, "Of course you can live with us." I agreed, but it was more a passing comment than a thoughtful response.

We began building "our home" between the third and fourth year of our marriage. Kayla graduated from high school and went to college. I prepared to be a part-time empty nester, planning my new, mostly kid-free, life. What would I do? What new adventures could I have? Jay, an 8th grader at the time, chose that moment to put a stake in the ground. "I want to live with Dad." The adults started talking. Our plan was to adjust the custody arrangements and have him transition after he finished his 8th grade year. Jay, however, had other ideas. By January of his 8th grade year, Jay was living with us full-time. The new custody arrangements were put in place by March, and all of my plans went up in smoke.

Again, I gladly welcomed Jay, but it would not be honest if I didn't admit I lost something, and I grieved what I had lost. Jonathan's travel schedule did not change when Jay came to live with us. With the stroke of a pen, I went from planning exploits to becoming a full-time mom to my bonus son...immediately. Jay moved in over the weekend. Jonathan flew out on Monday. I drove Jay 30 miles round trip to school. Clearly, God's purposes differed from my plans. I needed to bring my thoughts, ideas, hopes for a new season, and my emotions, to the table for major renegotiation, with an immutable contract that will never change.

DID YOU READ THE FINE PRINT?

We sing the lyrics, "I'm no longer a slave to sin. I am a child of

"God," or "I am an overcomer by the Blood of the Lamb." We declare with vigor and gratitude, "I am a friend of God." We crown Him King and acknowledge His Lordship. What joy for those who belong to Him! On the other hand, have you ever thought about what that actually means for your life? I'll tell you what it means. God owns you, girl. He owns me. He calls the shots. He makes the rules. We get in line...or not. Our acquiescence is as voluntary as our disobedience; and both have consequences. God sets the terms of Kingdom citizenship and belonging. He's in charge and it's His purposes which dominate Kingdom culture.

In Him we have obtained an inheritance, having been predestined according to the purpose of Him who works all things according to the counsel of His will, Ephesians 1:11 (ESV)

It's a win-win deal for us; we have a wonderful inheritance. But, make no mistake, sign the contract and you agree to be ruled. A focused heart is under new management. A woman focused on God's will for her life, His love for her, and her desire to honor Him in her roles, can ill afford to lose sight of that. We are chosen for *His* purpose. There is a reason why you, deliberately and especially, were chosen to be in your stepchildren's life. And it's not only to give you a happily ever after with their Dad.

My bonus-mom friend, Summer Butler, author of *Blended: Aligning the Hierarchy of Heart and Home*, gifts us a reminder of God's will for our children, and our role in His plan for their lives. I'll paraphrase her: The point of our step-mothering is that, our children, rather than become children who call us their mother, become children who call God their Father.

I clamor for appreciation and applause: God calls me to turn a deaf ear to admiration and put the spotlight on Him. For me, and perhaps for you, that requires frequent meetings with the Lord. Transformation is not linear. Growth dips, swirls, and squiggles its way towards something resembling progress. When dealing with issues which have the potential for promoting self-congratulation, derailing plans, or menacing your heart, you will need to know how to renegotiate.

When we choose to love before being loved, we agree to submit to conditions set forth in the Word of God; conditions that are foreign to our natural bent. I will be the first to admit, I don't always like it. Until His way of life becomes more fully our own, we will always have to come back to the table. It is not easy to trade my thoughts or ways for His.

Although I've made a determination to get over myself, and stay over, it takes ruthless vigilance to keep my thinking and actions aligned to His word and will. Following His infinite wisdom stretches me beyond my finite insight. When the resolve to obey God causes discomfort to my flesh, which is often, I find myself reaching for control. Truth is, the first person my determination will make uncomfortable is me. Acceptance of that fact fosters resolve. Life on God's side of the line in the sand may be harder on our agendas but it is much better than the alternative.

I'm sure you have made the same assertions. But, how do we deal with the resistance lodged in our hearts?

OWNING THE EMOTIONS

I dealt with a variety of swirling emotions when we agreed to Jay living with us full-time. Suddenly, at a time when I was anticipating the freedom of having an empty nest, I was thrust back into full-time motherhood. At minimum, a 4-year recommitment to full-time mothering laid ahead of me. I was both resistant and excited. I repeatedly submitted my plans to the Lord. Sometimes, begrudgingly. Eventually I began enjoying this unexpected detour. Then we were thrown for another loop.

About two years after Jay began living with us, my bonus daughter came to us and said,

"Mom said I need to change my address to my Dad's address and live here."

Unlike with my bonus son, there was no conversation. No consideration for our thoughts. To me, it was a disrespectful unilateral decision about what would happen in my home, without asking me or my husband if we were fine with the decision. I was livid! I mean, pick up the phone and make a phone call mad, something I would never do under normal circumstances. Both Jonathan and I were very angry. Only concern for our daughter cooled our tempers. There was a person in this equation who needed us, and would not be helped by our anger. It was time to pray.

It is vital to maintain flexibility, and empathy, to extend grace to ourselves and to the people in our lives in any relationship, particularly in stepfamilies. Paul wrote in his first letter to the Corinthians:

> Though I am free and belong to no one, I have made myself a slave to everyone, to win as many as possible. To the Jews I became like a Jew, to win the Jews. To those under the law I became like one under the law (though I myself am not under the law), so as to win those under the law. To those not having the law I became like one not having the law (though I am not free from God's law but am under Christ's law), so as to win those not having the law. To the weak I became weak, to win the weak. I have become all things to all people so that by all possible means I might save some. I do all this for the sake of the gospel, that I may share in its blessings.
> 1 Corinthians 9:19-23

In context, Paul was talking about evangelism. No matter his personal state, he identified and connected with people where they were, so that he could possibly win them to Christ. Empathy served Paul for the sake of the gospel. Likewise, empathy serves us in our families.

Jonathan and I talked through our anger in private; our anger at being disrespected, and our concerns for our daughter. I needed to become like a daughter who was feeling lost and rudderless in this situation, so as to win a lost and rudderless daughter. To my great dismay, the Lord instructed me that empathy needed to extend beyond our daughter to include her mother, as well. It could not have been easy for her to come to that decision. Although she should have handled it differently, I imagine it would have crushed her to come to us beforehand. Ugh! I had work to do. My husband and I owned our feelings, left them at the altar, then set about "winning" our daughter and praying for her mom.

We need constant immersion into the grace of God to stepmom well. It is important to come back to the table, review the contract (the Word of God) and enter into negotiations again. The terms of the contract are enduring, forever settled in Heaven (Psalm 119:89), therefore we are not renegotiating the terms. Instead, we renegotiate with our self-willed carnality, causing it to submit to God's will. God helps us in our resistance and leads us back to Himself.

EYES ON THE PRIZE

I know very little about negotiating; in order to serve you well I turned to the experts in achieving winning outcomes in dire circumstances. I skipped the boardroom. Talented, capable, business-minded people who broker deals should be applauded, but I needed the insight of a different kind of negotiator to help with stepparenting. I went to the crisis negotiators.

Crisis negotiators are trained to step into high stakes situations and communicate with reactive people who are threatening others or themselves. It is easy to react when dealing with difficult circumstances. However, thoughtless reacting will often have horrible consequences. Had Jonathan and I immediately fired back at my stepkids' bio mom, we would have escalated the situation, becoming adversaries aligned against her, rather than allies in a co-parenting situation.

Crisis negotiators use learned skills to de-escalate tension, change outcomes, and move the troubling individual towards help and safety. Stepmoms with hearts focused on the King's intention for their families, can learn to do the same. However, when we become the antagonist in our own story, there might not be anyone around to abate our out-of-control emotions. It's crucial we learn to de-escalate our own tension and emotions during critical moments. The bible opens the curtain on a tortuous time in Jesus' earthly life. We are allowed to examine His anguish, and by it, learn to manage our own inner warring.

> *Then Jesus went with his disciples to a place called Gethsemane, and he said to them, "Sit here while I go over there and pray." He took Peter and the two sons of Zebedee along with him, and he began to be sorrowful and troubled. Then he said to them, "My soul is overwhelmed with sorrow to the point of death. Stay here and keep watch with me." Going a little farther, he fell with his face to the ground and prayed, "My Father, if it is possible, may this cup be taken from me. Yet not as I will, but as you will." Then he returned to his disciples and found them sleeping. "Couldn't you men keep watch with me for one hour?" he asked Peter. "Watch and pray so that you will not fall into temptation. The spirit is willing, but the flesh is weak." He went away a second time and prayed, "My Father, if it is not possible for this cup to be taken away unless I drink it, may your will be done." When he came back, he again found them sleeping, because their eyes were heavy. So he left them and went away once more and prayed the third time, saying the same thing. Then he returned to the disciples*

and said to them, "Are you still sleeping and resting? Look, the hour has come, and the Son of Man is delivered into the hands of sinners. Rise! Let us go! Here comes my betrayer!"
Matthew 26: 36-46

Luke, author of the Gospel of Luke and the book of Acts, being the science minded, investigative, physician he was, wanted to detail for us how close to the precipice Jesus stood that night. He adds this detail to the Gethsemane narrative:

An angel from heaven appeared to him and strengthened him. And being in anguish, he prayed more earnestly, and his sweat was like drops of blood falling to the ground.
Luke 22: 43-44

Have you ever noticed how raw, honest, and relatable God is? That word *anguish* is much more severe than mere sorrow. In the King James translation, the word is translated *agony*. The Greek word is *agonia*. It is defined as severe mental struggles and emotions, a struggle for victory. He is familiar with the intense conflict that exists between our resistance and aspiration to obey God, the Father.

There actually is a medical term for what Jesus experienced that night in the garden. It is called, *hemathidrosis*. It's a rare medical phenomenon in which a person actually exudes blood from every sweat gland in their body. Each sweat gland has a small capillary that surrounds it. In hemathidrosis, extreme physical and emotional stress, and agony, causes the capillaries to rupture. The person begins to sweat blood.

Jesus' night in the Garden of Gethsemane was spent in negotiations with the Father and renegotiations with Himself. Jesus was filled with heartbreak, suffering, and gut-wrenching sorrow to such extent His body physically responded to the emotional torment. Sweat and blood gathered on His brow and fell to the earth in great, weighty drops.

The first task of a crisis negotiator is to lower heightened emotions. Out-of-control emotions cloud good judgement. The first step in renegotiating with your heart is to identify what's going on in your heart. What emotions are you dealing with in the moment? What has been triggered? What are your areas of struggle? Jesus owned His sorrow. He owned His torment. God the Son wanted to save us. Yet, in His flesh, He desired to save us utilizing a method different from the cross. He did not shy away from His feelings. With eyes on the prize, obedience and glory to the Father, and victory over Satan, sin, death and hell, He leaned into the agony. Then, He wrestled.

PREPARE TO WRESTLE

Jonathan and I did not pray a pretty, neat, Christian-sounding prayer with all the right scriptures notated. "Mad" is an understatement for how we felt, and I, for one, was not so willing to let it go the first time I prayed. I knew what God commanded in His word but I was trying to hold an appeal hearing in the Throne Room. I put in serious time on the mat.

Once you have identified and owned your emotions, ask the questions you might not want to know the answers to: "My Father, if it is possible, may this cup be taken from me..." Jesus was not afraid to entreat the Father; to ask for a different path, to ask the Father to, somehow, make the task before Him easier to bear. He held His own appeal hearing, inquiring, "Father, please change Your mind!" Call on your Heavenly Father. Talk to Him about what you desire that might be different from how He's directing you. It's okay. Negotiation is always part of renegotiation. Only, remember, surrender is the only option.

The intensity of suffering which laid before Jesus gave Him pause. He implored God for a modification to the plan. However, He approached the negotiation table with a humble posture of deference to the Father. "Yet not as I will, but as you will." Be ready to obey when you're given the answer. If not immediately, then eventually. Be willing to exchange your entreaty for His aim. I wanted to pick up the phone. The Father led me to His word, "A soft answer turns away wrath but a harsh word stirs up anger," (Proverbs 15:1). I rightfully wanted respect in my own home. I felt justified in demanding it. The only answer I could give, which would glorify God, was, "Not my will but Yours be done." Our quest for redress may make us feel good but it will blind us to what's really at stake.

What was it that engaged Jesus' emotions, attention, and passion that fateful night? He was in a battle to overcome His flesh and bow to the will of the Father. Heaven sent angels to strengthen His momentary frailty so that He could accomplish the Father's will; to die on the cross. What engaged my emotions, attention, and passion the night of my bonus daughter's announcement? I battled to overlook an offense, and the feeling of powerlessness at God's instructions to not address it. To assist me in obeying Him, God reminded me that I once prayed my stepmomming would glorify Him, reflect Him, and magnify His name. I prayed my stepmomming would bless my husband, our children, and their mother as well. God answered my prayer and presented the opportunity for me to rise to His purposes. His Holy Spirit strengthened me in my frailty so that I would act in God-honoring ways. On the wrestling mat, God answers your real need so that ultimate victory is won. God commits His power to assist our surrender.

The weightiness of what I wrestled over in my bedroom can in no way be compared to the eternal implications of what Jesus wrestled over in the garden. That being said, the principle is the same: When the Father is involved, there is more at stake than momentary relief.

PURGE

The next step in renegotiating with your heart is to make sure you get it all out. Unload the burden until the issue is simplified. Crisis negotiators keep their person talking until they can drill down to the heart of the matter. Simplified issues are more easily resolved. Keep talking to the Lord until you are done talking to the Lord. Three times Jesus withdrew from the disciples so He could pray to His Heavenly Father. These were not five-minute, blessing-the-food type prayers either.

The first round of talks lasted at least an hour (Matthew 26:40). The bible tells us in Luke, after He was strengthened by the angels the first time He prayed, He prayed all the more earnestly! God sent angels to strengthen Jesus, but Jesus still had some wrestling to get through. By the end of His third entreaty in the garden, Jesus was wrung out yet resolute. He unloaded His burden until there was nothing left to carry. His heart was clear moving forward.

I believe in being brutally honest in prayer. Why try to hide anything? He knows better than we do the secret thoughts, hidden motives, and deep-rooted issues. I purge in prayer. I cast every care I have upon the shoulders of the One who cares for me. I give Him my hurt at being misunderstood, and my confusion when it seems I've done all I'm "supposed" to do and nothing has changed. I unpack and unburden myself of ego and angst, demands and mistrust, hurt and skepticism. I admit to Him what He already knows; although my spirit says "yes" to His will, my flesh is often too weak. He responds with comfort, encouragement, and strengthening. However, He does not change His direction.

All of Jesus' wrestling and purging resulted in one thing, submission to death on the cross. If we are willing, all of our wrestling will result in submission as well. God is not an inactive observer of your life. He is the central participant. You are living your part in His story. He is interested and involved. If you seek Him regarding your ability to obey Him in your step-relationships,

He will send His power to help you. He strengthens us to die to willfulness, self-centeredness, and self-lordship.

LEAN

We frequently read of Jesus in the company of companions. The Garden was no different. All but one of His disciples went with Him to Gethsemane. When He wanted to venture further into the garden to pray, He took Peter, James, and John with Him.

Peter, James, and John were the same three disciples with Jesus on the Mount of Transfiguration. There they witnessed a glorified Christ speaking with Moses the Lawgiver and Elijah the Prophet. They heard the voice of Yahweh, coming from a cloud, affirm Jesus (Matthew 17:1-8). In the garden, to these same three, Jesus confessed, "My soul is overwhelmed with sorrow to the point of death." He continued, "Stay here and keep watch with me."

In the most agonizing night of His earthly life, Jesus wanted the nearness of those who knew Him best. He wanted His friends. Those who saw Him in His truest state. I did not wrestle alone. The match was mine, but I needed faithful companions to be with me. I turned to my husband when I needed reminders and someone to pray with me. I turned to a friend when I needed fresh ears to hear my struggles. God gave me people to lean on as I wrestled. Look around you? Who are the people you can confide in and depend upon? Who has God sent to point you back to Him when you struggle with the path He's laid before you? Who will pray for you as you wrangle your heart into submission?

When you're renegotiating with your heart, you will need to walk it out with a trusted someone. Walking in your Garden of Gethsemane is not an assignment for just any one of the many people in your circle. You need the extraordinary friends. The inner circle friends. The ones equally trusted with the glory God manifests in your life, and the issues you struggle to overcome.

When your heart is all over the place, you need the friend upon whom you can lay your turmoil and know it will be safe with them. You need the friend who will watch out for you. The one who will sit with you. Pray with you. Not take offense in you.

Sister grab that friend. Tell her you need her. Tell her of your struggle to obey God when it comes to loving your stepchildren. Let her pray you through your battle to forgive the insults and bless your offenders. Confess your need to realign your heart with God's will. Ask her to pray for you as God closes the deal on your heart.

WITH GOD, WE CAN

While writing this chapter, I participated in an online book study with a few friends about loving like Jesus. During our 6-week study, we consistently voiced our opinions as to why we could not love like Jesus. We mentioned everything from justice issues, to fear, to momma didn't teach me how. All are legitimate excuses which can be hard to overcome; none are reasons on which we can hang our hat. We laughed, we struggled, we dogged ear and highlighted every other page. The book, *Love Like That*, by Drs. Les and Leslie Parrott, is one of the easiest yet thought provoking books I have ever read. I had a few Gethsemane moments while going through that study.

Difficulty awaits you when you're loving before being loved. You will be tempted to throw in the towel. However, at some point you have to put the stake in the ground and make a decision: Father, not my will but Your will be done.

We find these prophetic Messianic words in Isaiah:

> *Because the Sovereign Lord helps Me, I will not be disgraced. Therefore, have I set my face like flint, and I know I will not be put to shame. Isaiah 50:7*

Isaiah begins this chapter with these words, "This is what the Lord says:"

The coming Messiah, speaking through Isaiah, goes on to lament Israel's sin (vs. 1), announces His authority over creation as the Word (vs. 2-3), and His intimate relationship with His Father (vs. 4-5). When we get to verse 6, He begins speaking of the torture He will endure prior to laying down His life for the sins of all mankind. In verse 7, the Messiah declares His resolute attitude towards what must be accomplished through Him.

Luke repeated these words in Luke 9:51. Of Messiah, now revealed as Jesus of Nazareth, Luke says:

> And it came to pass, when the time was come that he should be received up, he steadfastly set his face to go to Jerusalem.
> (KJV)

Jesus came to serve. He came to reveal our Heavenly Father. He came to demonstrate God's love. He came to destroy the works of the devil. He came to die. Therefore, He made up His mind that dying was exactly what He was going to do.

The emotions and plea in the garden, albeit keenly felt and sincerely asked, held no sway over His decision. He acknowledged the battle in His flesh but refused to allow His flesh to dictate His obedience.

The key to Jesus' dauntless resolve leaves us without the excuse, "Well, that was Jesus." There was a reason He was adamant in His pursuit of God's will. Hundreds of years before His advent, Jesus revealed the fuel for His unwavering march towards the cross: "Because the Sovereign Lord helps Me, I will not be disgraced. Therefore..."

Jesus could face the cross with dogged determination because He was convinced the Sovereign Lord would strengthen Him for the task; loving people, some who would never return that love, literally, to death. Jesus knew the Father would help Him.

Our Heavenly Father is with us, as well. Every step of the way. He plants in us a desire to fulfill His will in our stepmom role. The power that raised Christ from the dead is at work in us. His help assures our victory. His faithfulness feeds our own. When I am poised on the precipice of exhaustion, the Sovereign Lord refreshes me. He reminds me of my assignment to love my family. He energizes me for the tasks ahead of me. Therefore, you and I can set our face like flint, make up our mind to obey Him, and do it.

In a perfect world, simply making up our mind to love, and trusting the Lord to enable us, would be enough, but this world isn't perfect, and neither are we. Expect push back. As a believer in Christ, you become an enemy to the kingdom of darkness. The moment you decide you're all in and you're going to stepmom God's way, you enlarge the target on your back. No need to fear, just be aware; in addition to your own hesitations, you will have outside influences working against you. Your stepchildren will question your motives. Their family members will question your authenticity. Your friends will question your sanity, wanting you to be more self-protective. You will question your ability. Satan will question your God.

With all this questioning, your heart will experience an onslaught of assault, just, like our Lord and Savior, Jesus Christ. And, just like Jesus, God's purpose must become the final answer to every challenge to His will. His pleasure must become your "why." His desire to ransom your stepchildren, must calibrate how you relate to your stepchildren.

Here are a few things to keep in mind to help fuel your determination:

◊ Relationship augments reverence. The more intimately acquainted we are with God, the more significance He acquires in our eyes. When we see God, we will love Him. When we love God, we will obey Him (John 14:15). Spend time with the Lord. Increase time with Him when in a difficult stepparenting season.

◊ Our hearts do not have a bargaining position. We are called to submit. We do not negotiate with our feelings, our desires, or the opinions of others. To bring our hearts to the table for renegotiation is to submit to the Word of God.

◊ To the stepmom with a heart focused on obeying God, your specific family dynamics cannot dictate the bottom-line. An angry, resentful, jealous stepchild, or bio-mom, may make your obedience to God more challenging but that means God will avail you of more of His grace. You do not have to be in close relationship with them, but you are called to love regardless.

◊ Do not let bitterness steal your compassion. Keep your heart soft. Remember, your stepchild, and his or her bio-mom, are loved by God. You are in their lives to be a pipeline of God's love for them.

◊ Say this with me, *"How we are now does not determine how we will finish." The faithful God, who began a good work in us, will carry it on to completion, until the day Jesus returns* Phil. 1:6.

◊ If needed, escalate support by going to a pastor, a minister trained in stepfamily dynamics, or a therapist.

◊ Always, always, rely on, expect, and trust the Holy Spirit to instill His strength in your yielded heart.

My beloved Sisters, even as I write this chapter, I am praying for you. I am asking God to intervene in your family and situation. I am asking Him to root you in His love and give you spiritual wisdom and insight to be the wife and mom He called you to be. Better than me praying for you, Christ is praying for you. (Romans 8:34, Hebrews 7:25)

Robert Murray M'Cheyne, a 19th-century Scottish minister, said, "If I could hear Christ praying for me in the next room, I would not fear a million enemies. Yet the distance makes no difference; He is praying for me!"

The distance makes no difference! Jesus, the ultimate Intercessor, is praying for you. You will win the battle for your heart.

By the way, CrossFit is no longer part of my fitness journey. Thank you, Jesus!

TREASURE HUNT

Alright sisters, it's time to go on a little adventure. Grab your tools, namely your bible, journal, and pen, and let's do a little digging.

What one issue in your stepmom life causes your heart to disengage? What is the constant dripping that wears away at your intention to love your stepchildren before you are loved by them?

We undermine God's authority when we redefine His instructions to us. Where are you struggling in obedience to God?

Now, carve out some time, grab your bible, your journal, a pen, and find a quiet space where you can wrestle with God in your own "Garden of Gethsemane." Unburden yourself. Lay it all down. Don't go in with a heart to convince God of something against His word. Go with a mind to bring your heart into alignment with His will. Allow His truth to mold your heart. Ask for His Holy Spirit to help and strengthen you.

SACRED STRATEGIES

"I want you to approach with humility!"

Those words were impressed upon my heart as I prepared to have a difficult conversation with one of my stepchildren. I was emotionally exhausted and mad. Not a good combination. I had been ignored, given the silent treatment, deliberately excluded and more. My attitude in that moment was horrible.

I confess I have a penchant for independence, with a capital "I". I have to work at not making decisions before consulting God's word; work at not choosing my own way based on my limited vision of the landscape. I am a home-grown American girl, nourished on a diet of achievement, ambition, and self-promotion. It works for America. However, it does not work for the Kingdom of God.

MY MIND, MY WAY

My mother is a brilliant woman, with absolutely no sense of direction. I called my mother one day while driving to one of my bonus daughter's school from a direction I wouldn't normally travel. I asked her to look up the address on Google map and tell me if I needed to turn north or south onto a street. Silence greeted me.

"Mom, I'm at the corner. Which way do I need to turn?"

"I don't know. The map isn't telling me which way is North!"

Seriously directionally challenged.

The day, however, which is legendary in family lore, is the day my husband, my mother, our son (my bonus son), and I decided to go to the mall. My mother drove. I can't remember how we came to that decision, but I do remember most of us in the car thinking it was a mistake. On the way back to our home, we discovered our usual route was blocked by a street fair and we had to take a detour. My mother was not familiar with the area and needed navigation. By majority vote, I was elected to give my mother directions around the fair. Translation: my two guys ganged up on me.

We came to the end of one street and I told my mother to turn left. She checked for oncoming traffic, switched on her left turn indicator, looked left, then turned right!

Everyone in the car yelled out, "We said left! Left!" She laughed and replied,

"I know you said 'left' but my mind said go right!"

Have you ever responded to the Lord with some variation of my mom's words? I know I have:

"Lord, I know You said let it go but my mind told me I needed to tell them off."

"Lord, I know You said don't worry but my mind told me I had to figure it out this time."

"Lord, I know You said do not go, but my mind told me I could handle it."

Compared to the all-knowing, all-powerful God, who has already seen the ramifications of our choices, what our mind insists upon is of absolutely no consequence. Yet, we consistently reject instruction from Him. The writer of Proverbs warns: "There is a way that seems right to a man but in the end it leads to death" (Proverbs 14:12). We are know-nothings, whose every assertion of self-will signs our own death warrant! Still, we follow our own way. No matter how often I become a victim of my calamitous drive to direct my path, it is very hard to stop.

TRUSTING THE NAVIGATOR

When I trace my track record of success, going my own way has produced dismal outcomes. The end is death. To relationships, peace of mind, dreams, composure, some piece of my heart. I have yet to find blessed wholeness by following my own mind. Flailing efforts cause unintended harm to myself and others. I am grateful to God Who faithfully steers me back on course but, oh, the pain I could have sidestepped had I listened and obeyed in the first place. My radar for what is right isn't always true north. Consequently, I have developed a healthy skepticism of the leading of my heart.

It is tempting to believe we are incapable of self-deception, but the truth is, duplicity is hidden within the heart of man. I can be as wrong as a dog chasing skunks and convince myself I'm right. Self-deception bubbles up at the most inopportune times, leading in a direction polar opposite of God's will. He tells us to turn left, we're looking left, we have intentions and have made all indications of turning left. By some mysterious machination of the mind, we turn right. Sometimes the heart just wants to do its own thing.

This dilemma was at work in the Apostle Paul, too. To paraphrase him, "Although I want to do good, evil is present with me. So that I do the evil I don't want to do and the good I want to do I can't." (Romans 7:19-25) The Spirit of God has deposited the life of Christ in each of us but our old nature wages war against our new nature in Christ. Our old nature clamors for its way, independent of God. They say knowing is half the battle. To win, we're going to have to admit we are not the best authority on how to live life. We're going to have to keep our hearts submitted to the will and word of God.

None of the helpful tips I had read about being a stepmom in a newly formed stepfamily came to mind that weekend. I was supposed to turn left, but I turned right and was following my mind headlong into a serious blunder. Papa interrupted the agitation, calmed the storm brewing in my emotions, and spoke directly to my heart, "I want you to approach with humility!"

I paused as I made my way to our child's room and struggled to let go of my certainty of being right. Humility is not timid in its arrival. It boldly crashes against ego and demands nothing less than complete capitulation. God's authority broke through my dogged self-reliance. He, not I, knew the way to go. Thankfully, I listened and there was a detour in my intention.

PATH OF LIFE

David wrote in Psalm 25:4, "*Show me your ways O' Lord; teach me Your paths.*"

David knew God. David experienced God's love firsthand. He had felt God's power coursing through his body as he dealt with bears, and Goliath. He saw the wisdom of following God's ways, and the folly of going his own way. Still, on its own, his mind was incapable of devising how to honor God. He needed to be shown; shown by the Father who had demonstrated His goodness in all things. It was David's confidence in God's goodness which prompted his trusting "show me...teach me" plea.

My family has experienced our fair share of run-ins with misunderstanding, hurt feelings, and exclusion, on this road to genuine love and cohesion. Heck, after all these years we still do. Yet, God faithfully leads us through those murky waters. He is good, not just to David, but to me. He is good, not just to me, but to you. He is Almighty in your life and mine. He is our deliverer, our fortress, our Savior and God, in Whom we can place complete trust. He will show you how to be a stepmother who honors Him. He will teach you to act in ways which communicate His love. His ways open our hearts to the work of the Holy Spirit. Even in difficult interactions.

Despite my obstinance, He taught me His path of life for my family. I call them, "Sacred Strategies". Sacred because they have helped create an atmosphere in which we all feel at home. Sacred because they are cherished instructions from our sovereign King. Sacred because they remind Jonathan and me, and our children, that we are in a consecrated covenant in which we honor, esteem, love, forgive, and serve one another. It is my privilege to share a few of them with you now:

Approach with humility

> Therefore, as God's chosen people, holy and dearly loved, clothes yourselves with compassion, kindness, humility, gentleness, and patience. Colossians 3:12

Humility is maintaining a low view of one's own importance. Humility puts the needs of another person before your own. Humility elevates the needs and value of others in your thinking and actions without discounting your own. Thinking of yourself less rather than thinking less of yourself.

As I readied myself for what I thought was going to be a "talking to," God reminded me to put on humility. I was not to approach my stepchild demanding my rights but to clothe my mind with a perspective that viewed the needs of my stepchild as more important than my own. However, approaching with humility goes beyond positioning yourself in a lower place.

God dwells in unapproachable light and has every right to approach us with judgement and anger. Instead, He remembers we are dust. He considered the state we were in and remedied our lack. He humbled Himself, became one of us through the incarnation of Jesus, died for us, and makes His home in those who accept His gift of salvation. To approach my child with humility went beyond putting their needs above my own. It also meant to see that child's lack and rise to meet it as much as the Holy Spirit would enable me.

Approach ready to serve

> You, my brothers and sisters, were called to be free. But do not use your freedom to indulge the flesh; rather, serve one another humbly in love. Galatians 5:13

This second strategy encouraged me to approach ready to do something to ease the life of my stepchild. It's called parenting. For most women with biological children, it comes as natural as breathing. Every cry is met with food, warmth, a cuddle, or dry bottom. Service. Some moms become so adept at serving their children they eventually learn what is needed by the sound of their baby's cry.

As moms with children not biologically our own, we employ the same approach with our stepchildren. The only difference is that we are more deliberate (and age appropriate, of course). What was instinctive with our biological children is developed with our stepchildren. You can do it. Since God commands us to serve one another, He certainly has equipped us to do so. Our part is to approach both God and our stepchildren with a ready heart, pay attention to our stepchildren to see how we may best serve them, and capitalize on the opportunities.

Approach with the end in mind

If anyone serves me, he must follow me; and where I am, there will my servant be also. If anyone serves me, the Father will honor him. John 12:26

One day you and I won't be wives and mothers. One day we will no longer have employees to manage, bills to pay, or floors to clean (hopefully). One day, we will just be daughters, living in our eternal purpose, and standing with billions from every tribe, tongue, and nation of this Earth and we will worship the Lamb of God, forever and ever. It is that day for which we live. The day when we are where He is. The day when our work will pass before the Lord and, at long last, we will hear the words, "Well done, good and faithful servant!"

"The end" the Lord wants us to keep in mind is not a self-constructed vision of harmonious family life. He is nudging us to stay fixed on what really matters; to keep our minds focused on things above where Christ dwells (Colossians 3:2). Approaching with the end in mind is a simple reminder to live for what will last. Only what we do for Christ will last. Respond in the moment, but parent towards eternity. Resolve to commit all your parenting; bio, step, grand, adoptive, puppy, et al, to the Lord, knowing one day you will stand before Him to give an account.

Approach to understand

If one gives an answer before he hears, it is his folly and shame. Proverbs 18:13

At one time I believed the most important component of great communication was making sure I was understood. Unfortunately, I behaved accordingly. I interrupted, over-talked, over-explained, dismissed, defended, and more.

I thought if the person I was speaking to would only understand (meaning agree with) my perspective then everything would be just fine. It remained a mystery to me why, generally speaking, my attempts to communicate with the people around me failed miserably. Then God began dealing with me about how I hear.

Many of us listen with our ears closed, as much as our mouths. We're not hearing. We're listening only to reply. Usually, with a ready defense for our point of view. God wants us to go deeper than that.

The most effective communicators talk less, listen more, and listen with a goal in mind. They listen to understand the person in front of them.

To understand, we must remove the filters through which we hear so we can hear what's being said. Remove offense. Remove past experiences with the speaker. Lose assumptions. Take what is being said at face value. Do not look for hidden agendas and meanings. Depersonalize it so you lower the risk for defensiveness. Ask questions to gain clarity. Be open to the possibility you're not right about what is being said.

Then ready yourself physically to hear. Position your body in an open, receptive posture. Lay down all electronic devices. Lean in and listen for the underlying emotion.

Listen actively. Engage in the conversation. Paraphrase what is being said, i.e. "You sound frustrated at not being able to spend as much one-on-one time with your dad as you would like." Respond only after you're sure your child feels completely heard and understood.

Admittedly, I have not perfected this strategy. I easily fall back into old habits of communication. However, knowing I know very little about communicating well, helps me pay attention when it comes to speaking with my children. One of my bonus children told me, "It's easy talking to you because you take the time to listen." I'm making progress.

Approach looking for the win

So in everything, do to others what you would have them to do... Matthew 7:12

Even if you are the best listener, you will lose whatever ground you've gained if you misuse your new insight into your child by exerting power, control, or authority to ensure you win and they lose. Your child is not your adversary. They are part of your family. As we discussed before, you have an adversary, strategizing against you, looking for every opportunity to use your emotions, your family dynamics, even your children, to destroy your family. It is not your child. Stand your ground against your true enemy, the devil. Him, you fight tooth and nail. Your child, however, needs you to adopt a different approach.

"Sow in people's life what you want to reap in your own," is my paraphrase of Matthew 7:12. I don't want to be bullied, so I don't bully. I don't want someone using my words against me in a destructive way, so I give grace. Not every compromise can be easily reached, nor is it responsible to give in to every demand. You can, however, find a long-term mutual win for you, your child, and your family, even if it causes a little pain in the short term. Look for that.

Approach with honor

Be devoted to one another in love. Honor one another above yourselves. Romans 12:10

To honor someone is to recognize them; recognize their value and treat them with regard because of their value. Show admiration for what is admirable about them. Cover in prayer what is not.

This is hard to do when relating with difficult people, however, God did not say honor only those we like. Our honor of a person's intrinsic value has nothing to do with their actions or attitude. Honoring someone becomes easier when we remember everyone is valued by God. The baby born by the time you read this sentence is a soul loved by God. The person who hurt you most is someone loved by God.

Our spouses, children, stepchildren, family, friends, co-workers, even folk who feel like sandpaper grating our nerve ends, are not props decorating our stories. They are people with individual purpose and significance, who deserve honor because they are made in the image and likeness of God. Each has His signature of authorship. He cares about how we treat others.

Approach with baby steps

There is a time for everything, and a season for every activity under heaven. Ecclesiastes 3:1

Becoming a bonded blended family is a huge undertaking and you have a catalytic role. At times I feel overwhelmed thinking about all of the dynamics to negotiate and emotional landmines waiting to blow up. There are moments when I'm just over it. Sometimes I want to rush through and gloss over the real work needed to be a healthy blended family. That would be a mistake.

Like most things worthwhile, a bonded relationship with your stepchild happens over time...one step at a time. Don't rush anything. Slow down. You have a lifetime to find your rhythm, and it will change as new factors introduce changes into your family system, like a stepchild coming to live with you full-time, a child getting married, or a grandchild being born. Trust God, and your stepchild, to show you when it's time to step closer. Remain hopeful when you need to step back. Two steps forward, one step back is a dance move every stepmom will experience.

Approach with a deodorizer

A soft answer turns away wrath, but a harsh word stirs up anger. Proverbs 15:1

One reason your stepchild may struggle to return your love is that they are in conflict. No matter how old they are, or how bonded they are not with their biological mom, there will be times when they feel guilty for having positive feelings about you. Even more so if their mom grooms them with guilt. In other words, if she infers through her actions and innuendoes, or declares outright, that she feels threatened by you in some way, your stepchildren will batten down to make their mom feel less vulnerable.

If you find yourself in a situation where bio-mom is marking territory with your stepchildren or your shared grandchildren, do something brave. Let her win. Reject the invitation to fight. Leave the territory unmarked by your answering aggression. You don't have to bully your way to be acknowledged. Remember you serve El Roi. God sees. He knows. Instead, clear the air with the love of Christ.

The bible tells us, "For we are to God the pleasing aroma of Christ among those who are being saved and those who are perishing. To the one we are an aroma that brings death; to the other, an aroma that brings life. And who is equal to such a task?" (2 Corinthians 2:15-16). Your personality, sweetened and scented by the Spirit of the Lord, brings conviction to the hearts of those who reject Him, and comfort to those who love Him.

Misbehavior by bio-mom is your opportunity to influence your family...all of your family, for Christ. It is hard to do, but meekness is the greatest show of strength. Your quiet confidence in Christ will speak loudly and do more convincing than any argument from you ever could.

Approach with an open hand

And those who know your name put their trust in you, for you,
O Lord, have not forsaken those who seek you. Psalm 9:10

You might be familiar with my "becoming a mom" testimony. To make a long story short, doctors told me I could not have children. I spent years pleading, begging, praying, and bargaining with God. Others prayed for me. Still no pregnancy. One day I finally handed over my desire. "Father, I give up. If You don't want me to be a mom, I accept Your will for my life," I prayed. A few months later, I was expecting Kayla.

There are times when we are in danger of creating an idol of our desires. They become so important they begin to eclipse God in our hearts. Desires which are placed on the throne of our hearts don't begin as idols. Wanting a better job, better marriage, better anything, is not wrong. Wanting to be a mom is not wrong.

Wanting a loved one to be healed of cancer is not wrong. Wanting to be loved is definitely not wrong. However, these right desires morph into sinful demands when we attach proof of God's love, or our willingness to serve Him and others, to their fulfillment.

On behalf of our Father, I'm going to ask you the question He has asked me when my desires border idolatry, "Am I, alone, enough?" When He is enough to satisfy our souls, we release our wants, even the desire to be loved, to Him. When He is enough, we trust Him with the outcome. We clearly see control's sleight of hand and no longer fall for its tricks.

This strategy, more than any other, brought an amazing depth of freedom to my stepmomming. The more I gave up and in, the more joy I found in "just loving". As I loosened my grip on my desires, I found my desires fulfilled in my Heavenly Father. Alone. Letting go lightened that false sense of obligation to make something happen. Letting go gives our hearts permission to thrive. Dear sisters, let go and trust God with your family relationships. Open your hands and give up your dreams to Him. He never disappoints.

Approach with expectation

For surely there is a latter end, and your hope and expectation shall not be cut off. Proverbs 23:19

"Thank you. Really, thank you for everything you do for me. I love you." Those were the words our son (my stepson) texted to me after I met him at the tuxedo store to pick up his tux for prom. By the time he graduated high school, he had been living with us for 4 ½ years and had truly become the son of my heart. I tried not to cry as he joked and posed and prepared for new chapters in his life. When I left the mall, I reminded him I was proud of him and grateful to be in his life. He responded with the text above. I cried then.

I married Jonathan with eyes wide open. We had a pretty complicated family structure coming together; mine, his, and his stepdaughter who is the older bio sister to his bio children. I knew there would be challenges and major adjustments. I had hesitations, trepidations, and questions. Lots and lots of questions. However, I had Someone bigger than all of that. I took my hesitations, trepidations, and questions to Him. His answer was, "Put your hope in Me." Here we are years later. Like David, I can say, I would have fainted unless I believed I'd see the goodness of the Lord in the land of the living. (Psalm 27:13) Expectation kept me in the game. It kept me in fighting form. It kept me loving. It kept me praying. It kept me saying, "Yes" to everything God asked of me. And it keeps me doing so. Every morning an untapped brand-new reserve of love and mercy awaits us. Commit your family to the Lord, trust Him, watch Him work, and expect to see the goodness of the Lord in your life as well.

The day I spoke with my bonus daughter could have ended disastrously. Instead, that day laid the foundation for what is now a beautiful, mutually enjoyable and loving relationship. I don't know how the story of your family ends, but I know Who is at the beginning, end, and woven into every sentence written about your life. His goodness has been proven over and over again. I also know everything is going to be alright because He is there. Better than alright.

TREASURE HUNT

Alright sisters, it's time to go on a little adventure. Grab your tools, namely your bible, journal, and pen, and let's do a little digging.

There were several strategies we briefly reviewed in this chapter. Let's plumb the depths of one of them. Ask God to direct you to the strategy on which He would like you to focus.

Once that strategy has been identified, find 2 scriptures which support the main theme of the strategy.

List practical ways in which you can begin to implement this strategy into your stepparenting.

Choose one item from your list which you will incorporate immediately. Pray and commit your plan to the Lord, ask Him for His direction and wisdom in implementation.

STURDY LOVE

Carly watched her stepson storm out the door. She had a feeling it was for good this time. The relationship between her husband and Steve was stretched thin, which did not bode well for her own relationship with her stepson. If she were honest, she could not blame her husband. Steve barely tried in school, the police had called them several times, and they'd found marijuana in his room. He rarely talked to them. When he did, he spoke in one syllable grunts. The most recent infraction of the rules was the worst. Carly, and her husband Derrick, arrived home to find a strange car in the driveway. The house was dark. Derrick told Carly to wait in the car while he checked things out. Five minutes later a scantily clad young lady ran out the house, jumped in the car and took off. Carly walked in her home to find Derrick and Steve in a horrible yelling match. She laid her hand on Steve's arm to get his attention. When he jerked his arm away, he threw Carly off balance and she fell. Everything stopped.

At the time this incident occurred, Derrick and Carly had been married 13 years. She became Steve's stepmom when he was just four years old. He was a sweet, loving, and respectful boy. Derrick had full custody of Steve. His mother had been largely absent for 10 years of his life. Carly was the only Mom Steve had really known. She attended parent-teacher conferences, sporting events, took him to doctor appointments, cooked his favorite foods, and hugged away hurts. Steve enjoyed the attention of a loving mother until he turned 15. Along with new friends, Steve acquired a new attitude. Surly. Aggressive. At that point, he refused to go back to the youth group at church.

Carly and Derrick prayed. They imposed punishments. They took Steve to speak with the pastor. They took him to speak with a counselor. They went to family counseling. Derrick spent one on one time with Steve. At 16, Steve announced he was an atheist. He stopped calling Carly, "Mom" and began addressing her as "You" or "Her." Now a 17-year-old senior, two months from graduation, Steve wanted out from under his parent's authority, in every way.

After Carly fell, Steve packed a bag and ran from the house. She looked at Derrick. He told her, "Let him go." Steve did not return. Carly prayed.

WIMPY, WIMPY, WIMPY

I have talked to many parents who were aware of their children's transgressions but refused to confront them, refused to hold them accountable. Instead, they tolerated wickedness. I have talked to parents who justified disrespect because their child was devastated over a divorce. I have talked to stepmoms frustrated by husbands who withheld discipline because they did not want to spoil their weekend parenting time with actual parenting. I have cringed at demanding, entitled adults who had never endured the consequences of their behavior. It is not pretty.

Melonie's voice dropped to a whisper. "Kyle doesn't get it. I'm tired of being the bad guy, but if I don't step up his son will walk all over me." She continued, "Kevin called me a hag, again. Kyle keeps telling me to be patient, that I will win him over. I'm not interested in winning him over at this point. Kevin is turning into a dangerous person. Kyle has no clue what he's helping his son become!"

A woman I know refused to acknowledge the truth about her two youngest children. Rather than rebuke, correct, or allow consequences to play out, she excused and rescued. When she had indisputable proof of drug use, she denied it. She was easily satisfied with glossed-over answers because she feared the truth. Her children never took responsibility for their lives. They both died from drug related causes.

If you asked Kyle, or the woman I know, or any of the parents grouped above, they'd insist they love their children, wanted the best for them, and wanted them to succeed. They are slightly mistaken. They do love their children and want the best for them, but their inaction indicates an impotent love, inadequate to support the formation of good character. Their parenting is inclined more towards their own comfort than the good of the children they loved. I know it sounds harsh but it's true. They swallowed lies to condone poor parenting. These lies protected the abhorrent behavior of children and appeased the conscience of parents. In the case of one of the people mentioned, with deadly ramifications.

Wimpy, weak-kneed love is the type that will not rise to aversion to sin, that will not inconvenience itself. Just enough to be kind; not enough to be courageous. God's love, the kind of love you and I are called to demonstrate, is something altogether different.

Paul wrote in Romans:

> Love must be sincere. Hate what is evil; cling to what is good.
> Romans 12:9

Paul uses a strong word here. It is the Greek word, apostygountes. The word implies intense, violent hatred. God's love is patient, kind, thoughtful, humble, and everything else listed in 1 Corinthians 13, but don't let that lull you into a faulty belief that it pulls punches. Real love stands in direct opposition to sin. It sees sin for what it is; a threat to the liberty and wholeness of the person loved. Agape love's intense and violent hatred for evil, sin, and disobedience compels it to speak up, step in, act. It is compassionately dedicated to the good of the loved one. Agape is sturdy, substantial, and true.

HEFTY, HEFTY, HEFTY

Sturdy love shows up in dilemmas. It lights the way in predicaments. Even offense will not turn off the spigot of sturdy love. Sturdy love cherishes the offender despite offense. It sticks without being weak. It is responsible and sacrificial, truthful and grace-filled, welcoming yet uncompromising. Sturdy love confronts immoral, inappropriate behavior, not for the sake of pride or hurt feelings, but because the one practicing the behavior is trapped by their sin. Sturdy love provokes us to pray boldly while we are hurting. Cry and believe. Enforce consequences and forgive. Hope while we wait. Do good even when sinned against. It is how God engages and rescues sinners.

Focused stepmoms are compelled, motivated, and led by God's love...sturdy love (2 Corinthians 5:14).

Carly possessed sturdy love. She could not afford to get lost in the weeds. She and Derrick held steady through those turbulent years with Steve. Carly especially held fast to hope in the Lord. She kept her focus on what mattered; Steve's character, integrity, and soul. She insisted Steve treat her with respect without forcing her presence. She and Derrick doled out appropriate consequences. When the police stopped Steve the second time, his parents made a decision to let him stew in jail before picking him up. When Steve walked out the door, Carly did not give in to despair. Her stoicism the day he left had nothing to do with helplessness, nor hopelessness. She wasn't wringing her hands. Hers was a love reinforced by faith in the God who loved Steve more than she or Derrick ever could. She simply gave up.

GIVING UP THE RIGHT WAY

There was nothing else I could do. I was exhausted by the contention in my home. I had neither the mental capacity, nor the emotional energy, to pump myself up for another round with the stranger under my roof. I prayed, yet saw no improvement in the circumstances. God asked me to die to self. It seemed as if my first husband could do whatever he wanted, without any conviction from the Holy Spirit. Wretched woman that I am, I was tired of obeying God in a complicated and nasty situation. It was time to tap out. I laid across my bed one morning and prayed, "God, I give up! I can't do this anymore." That was it. Eloquence necessitated energy I did not have. I'm sure the Lord understood exactly what I meant because 20 minutes later I got a phone call from a friend:

"You breezed across my mind. The Lord told me to call you and tell you, 'Don't give up!'"

Tears streamed down my face. The Father heard me and answered. My strength was renewed as I released emotions and weariness.

A few months later, I awoke with a start at 3:00 a.m. Immediately I heard the Spirit of the Lord speaking to my heart,

"I want you to put Kayla on the altar and do not pick her up."

What?! I blubbered and howled like a wounded animal for two to three hours. I remember responding, "But, if I don't protect her, who will?" Heaven's answering silence did nothing to comfort my heart. I knew what He asked of me. To give her up. To Him. In more than a metaphorical sense where I acknowledge Him but maintain control in my parenting. Like Hannah's Samuel, Kayla was my miracle child, my gift from the Lord. And like Hannah, I had boldly promised she would belong to the Lord from my womb. Now, He was asking me to fulfill my commitment. He wanted me to trust Him with her. Trust her care to Him. Relinquish control during a time when I felt Kayla needed my protection more than at any other.

Red, swollen eyes, and a nose rubbed raw greeted me in the mirror that morning, along with a tenuous surrender. I gave Kayla up. I had to do it repeatedly. Giving her up meant that my natural instinct had to be filtered through God's word and direction. Giving her up meant that I had to allow the fallout of her father's actions to play out without buffering. Giving her up to God meant, keeping my eyes focused on God's purposes, and keeping her eyes focused on God's goodness, despite the upheaval happening around her. It meant praying, always.

Don't give up. Yet, give up.

Are you dealing with a difficult child in this season of your stepfamily life? Are you experiencing escalating disrespect? Has your child's behavioral or emotional challenges seized your peace? Tore at your marriage? Are you exhausted? Feel like you've done everything you can think to do? It might be time to give up. Not on your child. Please do not give up on your child or on your hope in Christ for deliverance, and healing. Rather, give your child up to God. The only One who can save, heal, and transform.

Giving up is not an act of defeat. It is an act of worship.

TOUGHENING UP
Someone very close to my mother once said to her, "If you love me, you'll agree with me." This person was hurting people around him, including my mother. He lied to cover his misdeeds. He refused to meet his obligations and responsibilities. He justified his actions and attitudes. My mother challenged him on several fronts. He responded with, "If you love me, you'll agree with me He thought love equaled unquestioned compliance with everything he wanted to do. If you disagreed with him, it was because you disliked him. Not what he was saying or doing. Him. It never occurred to him that my mother confronted him because she loved him. She saw the path his thinking had laid out before him; a path that would lead him to destruction. He didn't listen."

My mother was right.

It was hard for my mom to watch this person she loved make choices she knew was going to end badly for him. She lovingly refused to rescue him from truth just to appease his ego. Love refuses to give a person license to sin, mistreat others, or remain unchallenged.

To effectively confront any sin and misbehavior we see in our stepchildren, yet remain openhearted towards them, we need a clear understanding of love and justice. We need to experience God's love and have a sense of His wrath. The justice of God is as rooted in His nature as is His love (Psalm 89:14). God is love and God is justice. Long before the two converged on the cross, God revealed this dichotomy in His nature on another hilltop.

> And He passed in front of Moses, proclaiming, "The Lord, the Lord, the compassionate and gracious God, slow to anger, abounding in love and faithfulness, maintaining love to thousands, and forgiving wickedness, rebellion and sin. Yet He does not leave the guilty unpunished; He punishes the children and their children for the sin of the parents to the third and fourth generation." Exodus 34:6-7

By the time we get to the 34th chapter of Exodus, Moses had experienced God in a burning bush, participated in His miraculous delivery of Israel, and led the burgeoning nation, which God called His own people, to the borders of their promised land. Moses knew God, face to face. His relationship with God was so unique, to this day Moses is revered and known as the great law giver. Yet, he hungered for a deeper connection and intimacy with God. He asked God to show him His glory. God told Moses He couldn't see His face and live. However, He agreed to cover Moses' eyes, pass by and allow Moses to see His backside. As God passed by Moses, He described Himself. "I forgive, love, am compassionate and gracious. I also punish and correct. I am a righteous judge."

God's wrath and love complement each other. His love satisfied His wrath through Jesus' death on the cross. His righteous wrath magnifies His great love. In God, compassion and justice, love and wrath, are inextricably intertwined. Without justice, compassion is stripped of its wonder. Without compassion, justice is stripped of its redemption.

What does this mean for us, parenting in tough situations? A Stepmom focused on loving while waiting to be loved dispenses a Holy Spirit led mixture of both. Steady compassion. Sturdy assessment.

THE END GAME

I recently read an anonymous quote: "Chastening love is controlled by a loving heart". God, tells us about Himself:

> As many as I love, I rebuke and discipline, be zealous therefore and repent. Revelation 3:19

We do much harm to our children when we model a Jesus who asks very little, delivers from nothing, and whose love tolerates almost anything, even sin. God chastens us when He sees us going the wrong way because He loves us. He uses circumstances and consequences to discipline His children. It might cause temporary pain, sorrow, and tears, but God does not hate the child He disciplines. His discipline corrects wrong attitudes and mindsets. His discipline changes our heart and our intentions. That change of attitude causes us to change our behavior, repent, and turn back to the Lord. His discipline brings righteousness and peace into our lives.

Likewise, God uses parents, stepmothers included, to correct behavior in the children He has given us to influence. Unless that correction is encased in love it will never lead to the desired result; changed hearts demonstrated by changed behavior. This is what we're after in the lives of our stepchildren. Hearts changed, repentant, turning back to God. I wrote in my previous book, "Joyful, Joy-full:"

> We can be both pleasant and dangerous. We can be compassionate without conforming. Our faith is threatening but we are loving. Our faith has standards, but we are gracious. Our faith is persuasive, but we are open. Our faith confronts, but it also liberates."

Our faith challenges sin, but it frees the sinner. This duality of positions is amazing to see demonstrated in a woman's stepmomming.

Steve had been gone for two years. He dropped out of school, got his GED and took off for parts unknown. Carly prayed for him. The few times he called spewing remorse and venom, it was Carly who prayed over the phone, then hung up. As hard as it was, she refused to send requested money, refused to invite him home. She hoped for him and trusted God with him. One day the doorbell rang. Carly opened the door to find Steve, bag in hand, shame etched on his face. There was also something else in his eyes; a hint of repentance, and a spark of welcome.

Carly pulled him into a motherly squish. No condemnation. Steve laughed and hugged her back. Drawn by his wife's soft sniffling, Derrick came to the door. He stopped short as he took in the scene before him. Steve looked up into his father's eyes, and said, "Dad, I'm so sorry."

Some five years after Steve returned, their relationship is filled with laughter, acceptance, grace-filled correction, and understanding. They talked, cried, and fought their way back to each other. Revelations caused a great deal of pain for everyone. Yet, they hung in there with each other.

The second time Steve moved out it was with celebration and pride as his Dad and stepmom watched him pull out of the driveway.

LIVING WITH A STURDY LOVE

Any stepmom intent on embracing sturdy love faces huge emotional hurdles. At times, you will feel like the poster child for Wicked Stepmothers Anonymous. At times, you will be treated like that. Nonetheless, if we're serious about loving our stepchildren out of enslavement to deep patterns of selfishness, sin, and pride, we will find the courage to cleave to parenting with a sturdy love, and the boldness to take the first steps of faith. It is not easy, but it is doable by the grace of God.

I have learned how to remain tenderhearted, yet honest, about what I'm observing in my children. I'd like to reinforce your desire to embrace sturdy love with what has helped me grow in this area:

Protect your peace

Paul wrote in the 4th chapter of Philippians: Do not be anxious about anything, but in every situation, by prayer and petition, with thanksgiving, present your requests to God. And the peace of God, which transcends all understanding, will guard your hearts and your minds in Christ Jesus. (4:6-7)

God's peace comes to defend and escort your heart and mind through troubling, aggravating, and noisy circumstances. Protect the safe space His peace creates for you. Do not allow the actions and words of others to destroy your peace. That may mean removing yourself physically when behavior causes you to react in sinful ways.

Be honest about sin.

Galatians 6:1 tell us: Brothers and sisters, if someone is caught in a sin, you who live by the Spirit should restore that person gently. But watch yourselves, or you also may be tempted.

There is everything right about calling sin, sin. It's only when we recognize the truth about what is trapping our children that we can be effective in the loving actions we take, and prayers we pray on their behalf.

Realize that seasons come to an end.

In Romans 12:12 Paul wrote: Be joyful in hope, patient in affliction, faithful in prayer. Here, Paul reminds us we have a reason to be joyful, patient, and faithful. God is faithful. He answers prayers and delivers us out of painful circumstances. Whatever hardship you're experiencing right now in your family is not the end of your family's story.

Someone loves this child more than you do.

Isaiah 54:13 reads: All your children will be taught by the Lord, and great will be their peace.

As much as you love your children, as much as you long for their freedom and healing, God loves them more. He is working in their hearts. He is calling them.

Don't stop praying.

The bible tells us that the prayers of a righteous person are powerful and effective (James 5:16). Your prayers for your children invite the power of God into the issues they face. Keep praying and expecting to see the answers to those prayers.

Carry your own luggage.

You will bring a great deal of relief to your heart by remembering you are not in charge of anyone else's baggage, choices, or emotions. It will hurt you to see your loved one in pain and making choices which lead to horrible consequences, but you are not responsible to fix it. Neither are you strong enough to carry it for them. Carry them to the Lord.

Trust God

God is a promise keeper. The trustworthiness of His character is indistinguishable from the integrity of His word (Psalm 138). He promised to be with you on this journey. Everything you are experiencing is working for your good. Nothing is impossible with Him. Trust God.

Neutralize your interactions

Through prayer and research, I developed neutral and thoughtful responses for times I needed to confront behavior in my children without matching energy or dismissing feelings. These responses, and others like them, acknowledged their feelings, preserved both our dignity, and left the door open for a better relationship. Feel free to adjust for age appropriateness:

- ◊ Tell me why you feel that way. (This was especially helpful for times when I did nothing wrong but was a handy target)
- ◊ I can accept your perception of me but I hope one day you will trust my intentions.
- ◊ I need time to think about how best to respond. I will be back in XX minutes.
- ◊ You are free to not like me, but we must respect each other.
- ◊ Your anger is not my responsibility. (I did not use this response until my children were in their teens)

Celebrate what should be celebrated

All of life is lived in the tension between two extremes: birth and death, joy and sorrow, what is and what you long for. In the middle you will experience good times and bad times. Moments you will need to mourn, and times which should be celebrated. It's okay to show appreciation even while you are dispensing consequences.

Let Wisdom Speak

James is just one of many writers of Scripture who instructs us on how to have good and wise relationships: Who is wise and understanding among you? Let them show it by their good life, by deeds done in the humility that comes from wisdom. But if you harbor bitter envy and selfish ambition in your hearts, do not boast about it or deny the truth. Such "wisdom" does not come down from heaven but is earthly, unspiritual, demonic. For where you have envy and selfish ambition, there you find disorder and every evil practice. But the wisdom that comes from heaven is first of all pure; then peace-loving, considerate, submissive, full of mercy and good fruit, impartial and sincere. Peacemakers who sow in peace reap a harvest of righteousness. (James 3:13-18)

God's wisdom helps us handle the hearts of others with care. His wisdom is:
- ◊ Pure – His wisdom clarifies our intentions and motivations.
- ◊ Peace Loving – His wisdom prioritizes relational unity so that we do not alienate others with anger and strife.
- ◊ Gentle – His wisdom relates the truth with consideration for others.
- ◊ Humble – His wisdom acknowledges others and protects us from pride.
- ◊ Full of Mercy and Good Deeds – His wisdom helps us forgive and actively seek the good of others.
- ◊ Impartial and Sincere – His wisdom is objective and genuine.

Dear one, the love of God, on display in your heart, is sturdy; love tough enough to confront sin, yet tender enough to restore the sinner. As Jim Elliot prayed, I pray for you and me, that we allow the Lord to toughen our love and give us firmness without hardness, steadfastness without dogmatism, love without weakness.

TREASURE HUNT

Alright sisters, it's time to go on a little adventure. Grab your tools, namely your bible, journal, and pen, and let's do a little digging. Read 2 Samuel, chapters 11 and 12.

Why did Nathan confront David?
What techniques did Nathan use to confront David?

Now read Ezekiel 34:23-25
What is the end of David's story?
In what ways does this strengthen the hope you have for your own children?

PLANT YOUR HEART

In Matthew 13:1-23, to illustrate the four types of hearts which receive His message about the Kingdom, Jesus tells a story of a sower who scattered seeds on different types of soil. The first type was hard, and the seed couldn't grow. This represented someone's heart who's so hardened by sin, the Word of God cannot penetrate it at all. The second type was stony. The seed could sprout, but the roots could not grow deep. The stony heart listens, but is not convinced, so when trouble comes the Word withers away. The third type was thorny. The seed could grow but was choked out by the thorns that overwhelmed it. A person with a thorny heart receives the word of God, but distractions (riches, worries, unmet needs) and idolatry overtakes their heart, and they cannot grow.

In the fourth type of soil, good soil, the seed was planted deep, grew strong, and produced fruit. This represents a person who has heard God's word, received it with joy, and allows it to grow in her life. The Word sown in the good soil of the heart of a person who loves and obeys God multiplies. That's you, Sis. A blood-bought believer in Christ whose heart is full of the stuff which causes God's Word to grow. Today, plant the Word of God in your life, and watch it produce a bumper crop harvest in your life and family. Trust that His word will accomplish in your life His good intentions for your life.

I have a few scriptures listed to encourage your resilient hope in the Lord. Please take a moment to look over these scriptures. Pray over them. Memorize them and hide them in your heart. Ask questions of them. Sit with them. Ask God to open your understanding as you read. Most importantly, believe them, and ask the Holy Spirit to help any unbelief.

I will instruct you and teach you in the way you should go; I will counsel you with My loving eye on you. Psalm 32:8

He will call on me, and I will answer him; I will be with him in trouble, I will deliver him and honor him. Psalm 91:15

Commit to the Lord whatever you do, and he will establish your plans. Proverbs 16:3

Whether you turn to the right or to the left, your ears will hear a voice behind you, saying, "This is the way; walk in it." Isaiah 30:21

So do not fear, for I am with you; do not be dismayed, for I am your God. I will strengthen you and help you; I will uphold you with my righteous right hand. Isaiah 41:10

Because the Sovereign Lord helps me, I will not be disgraced. Therefore, have I set my face like flint, and I know I will not be put to shame. Isaiah 50:7

You wearied yourself by such going about, but you would not say, 'It is hopeless.' You found renewal of your strength, and so you did not faint. Isaiah 57:10

The Lord will guide you always; He will satisfy your needs in a sun-scorched land and will strengthen your frame You will be like a well-watered garden, like a spring whose waters never fail. Isaiah 58:11

You too, be patient and stand firm, because the Lord's coming is near. Matthew 18:10

Therefore, I urge you, brothers and sisters, in view of God's mercy, to offer your bodies as a living sacrifice, holy and pleasing to God—this is your true and proper worship. Do not conform to the pattern of this world, but be transformed by the renewing of your mind. Then you will be able to test and approve what God's will is—his good, pleasing and perfect will. Romans 12:1-2

Never be lacking in zeal, but keep your spiritual fervor, serving the Lord. Be joyful in hope, patient in affliction, faithful in prayer.
Romans 12:11-12

For everything that was written in the past was written to teach us, so that through the endurance taught in the Scriptures and the encouragement they provide we might have hope. Romans 15:4

Be on your guard; stand firm in the faith; be courageous; be strong.
1 Corinthians 16:13

But he said to me, "My grace is sufficient for you, for my power is made perfect in weakness." Therefore, I will boast all the more gladly about my weaknesses, so that Christ's power may rest on me. That is why, for Christ's sake, I delight in weaknesses, in insults, in hardships, in persecutions, in difficulties. For when I am weak, then I am strong.
2 Corinthians 12:9-10

Let us not become weary in doing good, for at the proper time we will reap a harvest if we do not give up. Galatians 6:9

Not that I have already obtained all this, or have already arrived at my goal, but I press on to take hold of that for which Christ Jesus took hold of me. Brothers and sisters, I do not

consider myself yet to have taken hold of it. But one thing I do: Forgetting what is behind and straining toward what is ahead, I press on toward the goal to win the prize for which God has called me heavenward in Christ Jesus.
Philippians 3:12-14

I know what it is to be in need, and I know what it is to have plenty. I have learned the secret of being content in any and every situation, whether well fed or hungry, whether living in plenty or in want. I can do all this through him who gives me strength. Philippians 4:12-13

May our Lord Jesus Christ himself and God our Father, who loved us and by his grace gave us eternal encouragement and good hope, encourage your hearts and strengthen you in every good deed and word. 2 Thessalonians 2:16-17

And as for you, brothers and sisters, never tire of doing what is good. 2 Thessalonians 3:13

I have fought the good fight, I have finished the race, I have kept the faith. 2 Timothy 4:7

See that you do not despise one of these little ones. For I tell you that their angels in heaven always see the face of My Father in heaven. James 6:8

His divine power has given us everything we need for a godly life through our knowledge of Him who called us by His own glory and goodness. 2 Peter 1:3

SECTION III

The Fruitful Heart

Praise God, Who has enabled me to love!

MARVELING MOMS

They sat around the table with varying degrees of shock and sadness on their faces. It was the day we decided to tell the children I had cancer. Some shed tears. Some sat in stoic silence. Questions were asked. I was scheduled to have surgery four weeks later. Followed by two weeks of doing nothing and four additional weeks of doing next to nothing. The children rallied around me. Only one of them lived at home at the time. One of them lives in the neighboring state. They rearranged schedules, sat with me, braided my hair, cooked, fetched, and cared. All of them. As one of them said, "You care for us. Now it's our turn to care for you!" Love planted. Love reaped.

There is a scripture, written in script, framed in an old, weathered picture frame, hanging in my office. It is John 15:16, which reads:

> You did not choose me, but I chose you and appointed you so that you might go and bear fruit—fruit that will last—and so that whatever you ask in my name the Father will give you.

It's a reminder to me that our lives are on purpose by design. Chosen. Appointed. For a reason. Our efforts yield a sustainable, Kingdom harvest, in the work we are given to do. You and I are parenting for eternity. Won't you abandon yourself to the Kingdom agenda attached to your stepparenting?

When we obey God, cooperate with the work of the Holy Spirit, and parent to glorify God, we will see Godly outcomes. I cannot guarantee those outcomes will take the form of family harmony, but, at minimum, you will experience godly contentment. Along the way, we are given ample opportunity to enjoy Him and marvel at His work in our lives and family.

TASTE THE RAINBOW

There are moments in my life when I am completely stunned by God's kindness, goodness, and attentiveness. He is extremely "other." Infinitely holy. Creator of the universe. The heavens are covered with His majesty. He set the moons, planets, and stars in place. All creation shouts His glory. He thinks a thing and it is so. His worth must be declared. If mankind stopped praising Him, the rocks would begin to cry out. Yet, He has fixed His gaze on mankind, generally. On you and me, especially, uniquely. I am in awe of I AM!

During the sojourn through my divorce, rainbows took on a particular significance. They symbolized a promise God made to me.

I sat on a bench one early evening by the riverbank at my favorite park. Loneliness and heartache shrouded my shoulders. I watched couples and families enjoying the waning sunlight. I could only watch them for so long. Turning my eyes away didn't help though. I spied duck daddies and mommies waddle to the water for a swim with their ducklings. I watched mated swans nuzzle and enjoy the intimacy of exclusivity. Even nature reminded me of what I was losing.

Having rained earlier that day, the lingering overcast sky did nothing to lift my mood. Suddenly my bowed head snapped up. There, right in front of me, was a humongous rainbow, painted on the canvas of the gray sky. It was as if I were sitting on a bench in a museum before a great mural. The Spirit of the Lord impressed these words on my heart,

"This is my promise to you that everything is going to be okay.

That comfort stayed with me for a few days. It wasn't long before another argument with my then husband eclipsed that riverside encounter, and I forgot about it until a few months later.

JOY ON THE BLIND SIDE

I drove down the street on the verge of tears. I was heading to my mother's after yet another horrific argument. Why wouldn't he just leave the house and leave us in peace? Why did he insist on remaining and wreaking havoc in our home? It was so bad; my daughter and I did everything in our power to avoid him. Sometimes that did not work.

Worship music played on the car's radio, but I could not hear it. The argument on repeat in my thoughts drowned out everything else. Eventually I sighed and prayed, "Lord, today would be a great day to see a rainbow." Maybe it was more a grumble than a prayer. I don't recall if the necessary ingredients to produce a rainbow were present in the atmosphere, but even if they were there was no guarantee a rainbow would appear. I do remember being discouraged after the argument.

A few minutes later, I reached the intersection of two major roads. I was in the right lane preparing to make a right-hand turn. Suddenly I hear, "Look to your left." There, in the sky was a rainbow! A reminder to me from God of His promise that everything was going to be okay. God was with me! God heard me. He answered my specific need to feel His nearness. The God of the universe was, and is, for me! I laughed out loud as joy exploded in my heart.

Oh, what a marvel He is!

COULD HE BE FOR ME?

If there is any question in your mind that God is expressly for you, please read the eighth chapter of Romans. Through Paul, the Holy Spirit begins the chapter with an amazing proclamation:

Therefore, there is now no condemnation for those in Christ Jesus, because the law of the Spirit of life in Christ Jesus has set you free from the law of sin and death.
Romans 8:1-2

After categorically laying out the struggles we have with obeying God in chapter 7, Paul starts chapter 8 with an amazing declaration. You struggle, you may fall, but you are not condemned! There truly is power in the blood of Jesus!

What follows that declaration are 37 verses of pure encouragement and life-giving truths about God's bequeathment to us who are in Christ. In Romans 8 we discover:

◊ We are free because Jesus fulfilled the requirement of the laws.
◊ We have life and peace when our mind is set on the Spirit.
◊ The Spirit of God lives in us.
◊ The same power that raised Christ from the dead gives Spirit-empowered life to us as well
◊ We are empowered by the Spirit of God to put to death the deeds of the body – we are no longer slaves to sin.
◊ We are adopted sons and daughters who get to call God, "Papa."
◊ We are heirs of God and co-heirs with Christ.
◊ Our bodies will be redeemed.
◊ We have the help of the Holy Spirit in prayer.
◊ Everything works together for our good.
◊ We are called according to God's purpose.
◊ We are foreknown.
◊ We are justified and glorified.
◊ No one can prevail against us.
◊ We have been given Christ and everything else pertaining to life and godliness.
◊ Who can accuse us? Who can condemn us? God has justified us through Christ.
◊ Jesus Himself intercedes for us.

- ◊ In everything we face we don't just get by. We conquer. We overcome. We war in battles already won for us because God loves us.
- ◊ Nothing, no power in heaven, Earth, or beneath the earth, no circumstance, or state of being, absolutely nothing will ever separate us from the love of God.

That's just one chapter in the Bible! God is for you, Sis. God loves you. God gives you everything you need to accomplish His plan and purpose for your life. All of Heaven fights for you. Even your desire to please Him comes from Him. It is mind-blowing to say the least. You are God's beloved and He will prosper you in your stepmomming. Your labor is not in vain. An abundant harvest for the things you've sown in faith, obedience, and love is coming your way. Go ahead and marvel at that.

PREPARE FOR YOUR HARVEST

We do not have to manufacture the breakthrough necessary to move from being measured bonus moms to being marveling bonus moms. It is the work of the Holy Spirit. In the same way the Holy Spirit is responsible for producing His fruit in our lives in increasing degrees of abundance, He also does the work of transforming. We are being made new every single day. Not by our might, wisdom, ability, or efforts, but by the Spirit of the Living God. Our task is to make our hearts ready for growth.

We cultivate the ground of our heart through prayer, meditation on the Word, time spent worshipping God, and obedience to God. We position. God does the work of growing His fruit in our lives. We do not actively grow it but we can know it's growing. Evidence of an ever-increasing Holy Spirit takeover is seen in our interactions with the world around us

A marveling stepmom knows her source of life is in Christ and Him alone. She discovers her identity and her cheering in Him. There is consolation for hurt feelings in Christ. In Jesus Christ we have buffering against misunderstanding, and victory over fear. A stepmom anchored in Christ discovers resilience. She is a woman nourished and freed by the Spirit of God, focused on glorifying Him in her parenting. She has been pruned by the Holy Spirit.

She parents up. Having abandoned the need for applause, her parenting is focused on obeying God in her role for no other reason than He is worthy of her obedience. She recognizes and understands His command to love, before being loved, is for His glory and the benefit of her family. She is consumed with loving God and loving others. She does not pressure her family to meet her emotional needs. She trusts God to satisfy her longing with His love for her. That stepmom will bear fruit.

The fruit-bearing stepmom parents up using four key habits: consistent display of God's unconditional love, interpreting difficult children from God's perspective, being a safe shepherd for her stepchildren, and a diligent, personal pursuit of God. In this section, a chapter is devoted to each habit, followed by a chapter titled, "Pour Your Heart", filled with biblical encouragement for flooding your family with love and truth.

I have been so excited to write this section of the book. Here we get to celebrate the praying and assessing you've done, the modifications you've made and the confronting and pruning the Holy Spirit is doing. This is the section in which we honor the work of God's grace in your life. I was frequently tempted to jump ahead and write this segment before completing the first two. Thankfully, my desire to walk with you through this book overrode my desire to get to this section. I waited, but it was hard. Let's wait no longer.

FIRST AND FOREMOST

The best way to describe Allen's response to Ashlyn at their first meeting is smitten. He was completely taken with her...and she with him. It wasn't long before they were planning their wedding. Ashlyn is a beautiful woman, known for her compassion and hospitality. The prevailing ambition in her life is to know and love God. She longed for marriage to a Godly man with whom she could share her life and who would make up for the absent father in her daughter's life. She felt she found such a man in Allen, a widower with adult children. Ashlyn and Allen spent the days leading up to their marriage dreaming of a life together. Ashlyn's daughter dreamed of new adventures, and new friendships. Allen's children, however, considered it the continuation of a nightmare.

Where others cheered at the wedding, Allen's children cried. When Ashlyn and her daughter moved into the home Allen shared with his first wife and children, Ashlyn naturally began redecorating. With every change she made, her bonus children grew more hostile. They called her 'Bash In' behind her back. Ashlyn's invitations to friendship were met with cynicism if not outright rudeness. Time after time, Ashlyn was tempted to stop trying. Time after time, the Lord strengthened her just enough for one more attempt.

Five years after their wedding, while at dinner with their family celebrating Allen's birthday, one of his children turned to Ashlyn and said, "Thank you for loving our Dad...Mom!"

It was a long road from 'Bash In' to 'Mom,' landscaped with both antagonism and kindness. The family progressed and regressed, steps forward and steps back. Acceptance and rejection. Answered prayer and waiting. Along the way, the Father showed Ashlyn how to wait in faith, with a heart ready to welcome. When asked how she remained consistent and loving through the see-saw of stepfamily blending Ashlyn replied, "By keeping my eyes fixed on the main thing."

LOST ONES IN YOUR HOME

The 15th chapter of Luke finds Jesus teaching in a crowd. Suddenly "tax collectors and sinners" approached the crowd. Jesus did not forbid them to come. The Pharisees and scribes start complaining. To the Jewish religious elite, tax collectors and sinners were far worse than belligerent stepchildren; they were the bottom of the barrel of Jewish society. Jesus did not avoid or even rebuke them. Oh, no! He welcomed them! Made a place for them. Received them. The Pharisees and scribes were outraged. Jesus told three stories in response to the prideful bigotry of the religious leaders. Those stories are collectively known as the 'Parables of the Lost Things.' The most detailed and well known of these is the parable of the Lost Son, or the Prodigal Son as it's more familiarly called.

Jesus introduces the crowd to a responsible, wealthy man with two sons. One of the sons, the younger, asks the father for his share of the estate. Every first century Jew listening to this story would understand the context. This son was essentially saying to his father, "Drop dead!" Jesus goes on to say the father distributed the assets to them. Both the younger and older sons received assets from the father.

The younger son, tired of living under the authority of his father, packed up his belongings and took off for the high life. After he spent everything he had, economic collapse hit the land. The bible says a severe famine. In a time when agriculture was a major industry, famine meant economic collapse. Eventually, he was hired to feed the pigs of a local man. Unfortunately, that was not enough to meet his basic needs.

In desperation, the son considers eating the carob pods used to feed the livestock because no one would or could feed him. The pigs were better off than the young man. He finally had enough of himself. He discovered, at the end of his self-rule, a life bereaved of companionship and resources. The now humbled young man made up his mind to return home, beg for forgiveness, and offer himself to serve in the home where he was once a son.

We may never know the pain of loving a child physically lost to us. However, in our roles as someone's stepmom, in all likelihood we have known the pain of loving a child emotionally lost to us. Living in our home, yet absent. Looking through us rather than at us. A loved family member who has barred us from fully expressing that love.

Ashlyn had bonus children who were lost to her. They were grieving their mom, grieving her absence at their upcoming milestones. Grieving the comfort and security of Mom and Dad together. To them Dad was moving on, forgetting Mom. Ashlyn's presence was not something they were willing to face much less accept. They used hostility, stonewalling, and criticism to, in effect, run away from home; until finally they stopped running and turned towards home.

FATHER OF LOST ONES

Luke writes in verse 20 of this chapter:

> So he got up and went to his father.

> But while he was still a long way off, his father saw him and was filled with compassion for him; he ran to his son, threw his arms around him and kissed him.

Jesus doesn't give a whole lot of detail about the time the younger son was away. We know the younger son went away, spent all his money on foolish living, fell on hard times, repented, and decided to go home and beg for mercy. We don't know how long the son was away.

We aren't told what the father did while he waited. We don't know much about his life in the interval. We only know how he responded when the wait was over.

Some bible teachers assert the father was desperately looking for his son because he saw him while the son was still far-ways off. I don't believe that. Jesus used the father in this story as a typography of Father God. God is not sitting in forlorn hope waiting for a prodigal's return. He is ready to receive a lost one turning in repentance from sin to Him. While they are making their way home, He meets them in welcoming joy and celebration. Still, God is omniscient. He knows when, or if, a lost one will return to Him.

I would like to suggest a possible scenario. This is not book, chapter, and verse, just the musings of an overactive imagination. We know the father hoped for the son's return because he kept his son's ring and robe ready and easily accessible. We know the father waited. He had no other choice. He loved because that was his nature. We can deduce he prayed for his son's protection. We know he was concerned because the servant noted to the older son the reason for the father's party was that the son was back safe and sound (v. 27). "Safe and sound" is the language of the concerned.

I think the reason the father's activity between his son leaving and returning is not mentioned is because the father did nothing out of the ordinary. Clearly, he continued to care for his estate, he still had servants and the means to throw a huge party. No, he was not twiddling his thumbs. He acted like a father. He kept doing what he knew was good to do.

Ashlyn acted like a mother towards her stepchildren. She was not their mother, nor did she attempt to fill the space in their lives left by their deceased mom. She became to them, like Paul and his co-laborers were to the Thessalonians.

> Just as a nursing mother cares for her children, so we cared for you. Because we loved you so much, we were delighted to share with you not only the gospel of God but our lives as well.

1 Thessalonians 2:7b-8

She cared for them. She shared the gospel with them in word and deed. She made their favorite dishes when they came to the house. She politely excused herself when she needed space. She gave respect. She confronted disrespect without counterattacking. She loved their father. She shared as much of her life as they would receive. She went to the Lord to refill. She did not watch the horizon for them while she waited. She loved, she prayed, she lived, and she worked. She kept doing what she knew was good to do.

FROM HERE TO THERE AND BACK AGAIN

It's tough to admit that non-fiction authors can stray over the hearts of their readers from time to time. In an attempt to be helpful, non-fiction authors can sometimes oversimplify ideas, and neglect the heart of the real-life person on the other side of the page. Most people have a long journey to get an idea, thought, way of life, out of their head and into their heart. It's easy for me to talk about the outcomes and steps. However, I would be wholly dissatisfied if, when you close this book, you only had a roadmap. My prayer and desire for you is that any truth you read leads to awakened passion in your heart; for God, for stepmomming in God honoring ways, and for living for God's glory. My desire is that the Lord will use this book to shorten the distance between your head and your heart.

Moving from head to heart is a journey that involves a deep look at motivation. Everything begins in the heart; the ruling center of a person, our conscience, our mind, will, and emotion. From the heart comes our desires, our driving force, our manners, and beliefs. The pricelessness of our heart is endorsed by the biblical warning to guard our hearts with more diligence than anything else we guard, because everything we do flows from it (Proverbs 4:23).

Jesus made it clear as day, He could care less about religious activity for its own sake. In His sermon on the mount (Matthew 5-7), He repeats the phrase, "You have heard it said..." followed by a law. He then places an addendum on the law by saying, "But, I say..." followed by a challenge to the listener's motivation. The Word unveils the intent of the word. This is the pilgrimage you and I are on right now.

Jesus said in John 8:32, "You will know the truth and the truth will make you free." Knowing truth is more than knowing what is right, accurate, or authentic. Ultimately, truth leads us to the Truth...a Person. Jesus revealed Himself to be the way, truth, and life (John 14:6). Knowing truth is knowing Christ. Then Christ causes truth to come to life in our hearts. When we come to know Him, His truth sets us free. Freed from and freed to.

He frees us from old patterns of behavior and thoughts. Jesus sets us free from the penalty of sin in eternal life, and the power of sin in our daily lives. He frees us from slavery to offense and misunderstanding.

He frees us to real life in Christ; righteousness, peace and joy in the Holy Spirit. He frees us to stand guiltless in the presence of Almighty God. He frees us to wholeness and new ways of being. He frees us to love without thought of recompense.

As we respond to His invitation with tentative steps of faith, He does the lion share of work. When you and I lean on Jesus, and surrender to His power to transform, He is the one who moves our faith from our heads to our hearts. We trust. He shapes. We bow. He changes. Ashlyn looked to and leaned on Jesus.

As fruitful stepmoms, through whom God blesses our families, our lives are laser-focused on knowing God and receiving His love. Knowing God, and receiving His lavish love, make obedience to the most important commandments, to love Him and others, an exercise in joyful reciprocity.

As Ashlyn waited, she dedicated her stepmomming to the Lord. She welcomed before being welcomed. Every act for her family became an act of worship to the Lord. The greater her intimacy with God, the more joy she found in her role. The tangible power of God in her everyday life fanned the flames of her faith. She relieved herself of the responsibility to make something happen. Her tension eased, she relaxed, and her stepmomming became an authentic expression of God's love for her family. The distinguishing qualities of fruit bearing stepmoms are intimacy and obedience.

SEE THE LORD

Time-travel with me, if you will, to the ancient kingdom of Judah. This is not a pleasure venture. The air is polluted with the sounds of wailing as people mourn the death of their great king. Most remember him as a leper, but some recall the victories, the affluence, and the relative ease that came with his reign. As we make our way to the center of town, the marketplace is subdued. Groups of people huddle together, recounting stories, exaggerating encounters, shushing rumors, and soothing fears. He had largely been absent these past few years due to disease, but they remembered and grieved. Then Isaiah steps in with a world-shattering pronouncement.

The 6th chapter of Isaiah begins with faith anchoring verses. They are a revelation of a God who is constantly enthroned, in charge, and worthy of worship. Isaiah writes:

> In the year that King Uzziah died, I saw the Lord, high and exalted, seated on a throne; and the train of his robe filled the temple. Above him were seraphim, each with six wings: With two wings they covered their faces, with two they covered their feet, and with two they were flying. And they were calling to one another:

> "Holy, holy, holy is the Lord Almighty;
> the whole earth is full of his glory."
> Isaiah 6:1-3

King Uzziah reigned in Judah for 52 years. You can find an account of his history in 2 Chronicles 26 and 2 Kings 15 (He's called Azariah in 2 Kings). He was a good king almost throughout the entirety of his reign. Judah prospered under his stewardship. He was strong, energetic, an excellent military strategist, a builder and planner. His exploits were known throughout the Middle East (2 Chronicles 26:5). At some point during his reign, he became arrogant, self-sufficient, and inappropriately assumed the duties of a priest. (2 Chronicles 26:15) The Lord responded by striking Uzziah with leprosy. He died in isolation, diseased and ashamed.

With that opening statement, "In the year King Uzziah died," Isaiah readied his audience for the gravity of his next words. Uzziah's death was significant. Uzziah, although he died tragically, was someone to be venerated. Isaiah and his fellow countrymen enjoyed the security and comfort a skillful leader brings to a country. The great protector was dead. What would happen to them? Whose reputation would keep their enemies in check now? Who would replace him? It would take an imposing person to eclipse Uzziah's stature. In the year the great King Uzziah died, someone more impressive happened to Isaiah.

"...I saw the Lord high and exalted, seated on a throne."

Israel had been looking to Uzziah, concerned about the state of current affairs, fretting over the king. Then Isaiah saw the King.. There was a stark contrast between the circumstances and the Lord.

Uzziah was dead. The Lord is alive. Uzziah was in the ground. The Lord is high. Uzziah's throne was exposed, subject to challenge and death. God's throne is invulnerable, exalted and majestic. Uzziah's throne was empty. The Lord is seated on His throne. Judah's king was no more. Judah's King is ever more.

"...and His train filled the temple."

Ancient kings wore robes with long trains to signify they were people of honor, dignity, whom others recognize with service and deference. The longer the train, the more noteworthy the person. God is so worthy of honor, and adoration, the train of His robe filled the entirety of the temple. No earthly king had a robe with a train which filled an entire temple! In the retelling of his vision, Isaiah distinguished God as a King in a class all by Himself.

Six-winged beings constantly fly around His throne. With two wings they cover their faces. They cannot endure the radiance of His holiness. With two they cover their feet, concealing themselves in acknowledgement of their unworthiness. With two they fly, continually occupied with the One who sat on the throne. Four wings used to express humility and worship, two used to express service and obedience. Isaiah trembled at their proclamation:

"And they were calling to one another: "Holy, holy, holy is the Lord Almighty; the whole earth is full of his glory.""

Never do the beings dare address God directly. They exhort each other with praise of the Lord while in His presence. The cry "Holy" is heard three times. In the Hebrew language repetition increases intensity. They declared God is as holy as holy could ever be. He is the holiest. There is absolutely nothing and/or no one more holy than He. His holiness will never diminish.

Not only they, but the whole earth glorifies Him. Everything around us shouts His grandeur and majesty. The glistening of moonlight on the snow-covered ground. The thunder of the ocean's tide rushing in. The dazzling grace of wildflowers waltzing in the breeze. All sing His praises. They must, for God is holy, holy, holy!

I want to encourage you to take a trip through the Psalms. Psalm 18, 103, 117, and 145 are great ones to begin with. As you read, note which attribute of God the Psalmist is applauding. Clap along with him. Gaze on the visage of the God of Wonders. The clearer picture you have of Who you are serving, the easier it is to stay focused on Him.

Christ, the visible image of the invisible God, makes the Holiest God approachable. Through Christ, you and I are invited to come near. Know Him. Experience Him. Beholding the glory of God brings everything into perspective. What was once insurmountable is now conquerable. Faith replaces doubt. Adoration replaces self-absorption.

As we contemplate the holiness of God, hawkish stepchildren become fleeting shadows in the light of His magnified presence. The only wise God, capable, eternal, the Source of all life, is the turner of hearts and smoother of rough roads. Bigger than painful interactions. Behold Him long enough and you will find yourself serving the people you were questioning.

Further in Isaiah 6, we discover Isaiah's response to the great King.

Made aware of God's holiness, Isaiah fell to his face in despair. His sinfulness became apparent. When we recognize the grandeur of God's glory, our only response is to bow. The slights of others against us pale in comparison to our slights against the King of Glory. Yet, God is merciful. He provided a remedy for Isaiah's sin; an angel touched Isaiah's lips with a coal from the altar to take away Isaiah's iniquity and purge his sin. God has a remedy for you and me; the blood of Jesus Christ, shed to take away our iniquity and purge our sin.

Isaiah was knocked for six by God's graciousness so when God asked, "Who will go to these people," Isaiah answered, without hesitation, "Here am I. Send me."

During her blended family adventure, the majesty of God captured Ashlyn's attention. She beheld the glory of God in the Son, Jesus Christ. She was amazed by the Lord's mercy. With her iniquity removed, and her debt paid, His pleasure became her primary motivation. Her response to God's desire to make Himself known to her stepchildren was "Here am I. Send me!"

IN FILLING FOR OUTPOURING

Friend, you are the daughter of a Father who makes us new and transforms and molds us into His likeness. When He looks at you, He does not see a bumbling, stumbling, girl, who sometimes gets it right. You do not frustrate Him. You cannot disappoint Him. When He looks at you, He fixes His gaze on His finished work; a daughter, conformed to the image of His Son, made complete in Him. He is alive in you and will bless your family through you.

I want to be a fruit-bearing step-momma. How about you? What if I told you there is a way to remain steady and strong through the instability which is stepfamily life; to bear fruit when it seems what you're doing is unproductive? The way forward is to get filled up with the Holy Spirit.

The Lord is really into filling: satisfying and replenishing. Psalm 81:10 tells us He fills our mouths with good things. Psalm 103:5 lets us know God fills our lives with good things. He fills the spiritual hunger of those who chase after righteousness. His unfailing love fills the Earth. He fills our hearts with His love. Most astonishingly, He fills us with His Holy Spirit...Himself.

I want to reiterate Paul's prayer for the Ephesians:

> I pray that out of his glorious riches he may strengthen you
> with power through his Spirit in your inner being, so that
> Christ may dwell in your hearts through faith. And I pray that
> you, being rooted and established in love, may have power,
> together with all the Lord's holy people, to grasp how wide
> and long and high and deep is the love of Christ, and to know
> this love that surpasses knowledge—that you may be filled to
> the measure of all the fullness of God. Ephesians 3:16-19

All scripture is inspired by the Holy Spirit, therefore, we can safely assert Paul prayed God's desire for us; that we would be strengthened by His Spirit, know His love, and be filled to the brim with Christ. However, we aren't filled only for the sake of being filled. Like most Kingdom matters, there is purpose tied to the filling.

I recently came across a YouTube video in which the video host held up an empty glass and asked the question, "How do you get rid of the air in an empty glass?" The obvious answer is fill it up. Whatever is poured into the glass, in this case, water, displaces what was in the glass, in this case air. However, water isn't poured into the glass just to fill it up. It is filled up to be poured out.

Luke records multiple accounts of God filling His people with His Holy Spirit in the book of Acts (2:4, 4:8, 29-31, 9:17, 13:9, 52). These are infillings, subsequent to salvation, which empowered believers to worship and to witness. The infilling of His Spirit displaces what is not like Him and replaces that with Himself. Like that glass of water, we are filled up to pour out refreshment.

Let's revisit Paul's letter to the believers in Ephesus;

> Do not get drunk on wine, which leads to debauchery. Instead,
> be filled with the Spirit, speaking to one another with psalms,
> hymns, and songs from the Spirit. Sing and make music from
> your heart to the Lord, always giving thanks to God the Father
> for everything, in the name of our Lord Jesus Christ.
> Ephesians 5:18-20

Paul writes to persuade believers then, and today, to develop a thirst for the Spirit of the Lord; experience the empowering presence of the Spirit of the Lord and be filled until there is an overflow of worship (sing and make music from your heart to the Lord) and witness (speak to one another...). Ashlyn's fixation on the presence of God, and His answering infilling of His Spirit, enabled Ashlyn to worship Him, to share the Gospel, and to love her children while she waited.

GETTING IN POSITION

The cancer specialists caring for me believed I had stage one cancer which had not metastasized. Consequently, they decided the best course of action was surgery. During the procedure I had to be arranged in a position that would grant the surgeon the greatest access to the offending tissue. They could have laid me on my back to perform the surgery, but that would have placed me at greater risk of exposure to the cancer, injury or death. They needed a clear path. The first thing they did, after putting me to sleep, was position me for easy access.

We are not the active agents when it comes to being filled with the Spirit of God. We cannot fill ourselves with the Holy Spirit. God, by His grace, does the filling. We can, however, grant Him greater access by positioning our hearts. We can clear the way to the core of who we are by incorporating spiritual disciplines into our lives. I know that does not sound glamorous, but exciting transformation happens in our hearts when we turn our attention to the Lord in expectation and consistency. The following are just a few ways in which we tilt our hearts towards the Lord for His infilling:

Ask: Luke records Jesus' words in Luke 11:13 "If you then, though you are evil, know how to give good gifts to your children, how much more will your Father in heaven give the Holy Spirit to those who ask him!" We have a good Father, perfect in all of His ways, who wants to give His Spirit. Want more of Him? Ask Him. He will not withhold Himself from you.

Obey: Obedience conforms our lives, thoughts, and ways to His life, thoughts and ways. Obedience aligns our hearts with His heart. Obedience brings us into intimate fellowship and friendship with Him. He shares His life with obedient daughters; a life characterized by harmony, grace, goodness, peace, righteousness, wisdom, beauty, and joy.

Prayer: Prayer is how we communicate with, acknowledge, and invite the activity of God into our daily life. Prayer focuses our hearts on hearing from a God who hears and answers. (Psalm 91:15, Isaiah 65:24)

Worship: Worship exalts God and acknowledges His worthiness. The Bible tells us God inhabits the praises of His people (Psalm 22:3). When we worship the Lord, He meets with us. We encounter His presence and experience the fullness of joy. (Psalm 16:11)

Communion: Adopt the habit of remembering and celebrating Jesus' death on the cross for our sins (1 Peter 3:18). It keeps us focused on the covenant lovingly ratified in the blood of Jesus.

Stillness: The Psalmist wrote: "My heart is not proud, Lord, my eyes are not haughty; I do not concern myself with great matters or things too wonderful for me. But I have calmed and quieted myself, I am like a weaned child with its mother; like a weaned child I am content." (Psalm 131:1-2) In stillness we learn to be contented by the presence of God. In stillness we come to know Him in the way He wishes to reveal Himself. I highly recommend the book *Invitation to Solitude and Silence: Experiencing God's Transforming Presence* by Ruth Haley Barton. I went through it with my bible study group a few years ago. It was a wonderful experience of spiritual formation.

Again, these are just a few of the ways in which we position our hearts for the infilling of God's Spirit. We also tilt our hearts through bible study, serving those in need, fasting, prayer walking, and fellowship. If you're interested in learning more, I recommend *Spiritual Disciplines Handbook: Practices that Transforms Us* by Adele Ahlberg Calhoun. For a realistic fictional portrayal of what granting access to the Holy Spirit looks like in our lives, pick up the bestselling *Sensible Shoes* series by Sharon Garlough Brown. You will not be disappointed.

The Father delights in giving us the Kingdom (Luke 12:32), everything we need pertaining to life and godliness, and making us partakers of His divine nature (2 Peter 1:3-4). He delights in setting us free. He also delights in making us co-laborers in His liberation of others. Oh, my friend, what an astonishingly generous God we serve!

MOTHER OF THE FOUND ONES

Reading the father's response to his returning son causes my heart to swell with devotion. There was no rebuke in the reception. No smug, "I told you so!" No punishing demotion. Upon his return home, the young man was immediately restored; position, rank, reputation, everything.

The father returned both the ring and the robe, signifying his reclamation of the son once lost to him; just as if the son had never sinned against him. The father received him with love and hoopla. He called everyone to celebrate along with him. This is exactly how Heaven received you and me when we returned to the Father.

Jesus says in Luke 15:10:

> "In the same way, I tell you, there is rejoicing in the presence of the angels of God over one sinner who repents."

Heaven erupted with celebration when you and I turned our heart towards God. We, who were once lost, without a home, or a name, were found and reclaimed. That's a reason for rejoicing.

Refocusing her attention on Jesus kept Ashlyn's heart tender and ready for the moment when her lost ones came home. Today, Ashlyn is Mom and Nana. Beloved, blessed, and wanted. She received, "Thank you, Mom," and quietly rejoiced. Cried tears of joy in private, but publicly did nothing more than hug her children close. She accepted the hearts turned towards her, without rebuke, chastisement, punishing, withholding or gloating. She fully embraced her bonus children and became mother to the found ones.

It is lonely waiting to be wanted. Yet, God meets us in the waiting, and while there, He teaches us to love children who act out of hurt without absorbing the pain of their hurtful actions. This means you're going to do a bit of limb-walking. It's scary out there on the limb. We have no strength on our own to do this, but I am absolutely confident we can do everything through Christ. Be brave, Stepmom: the fruit is on the limb.

TREASURE HUNT

Alright sisters, it's time to go on a little adventure. Grab your tools, namely your bible, journal, and pen, and let's do a little digging. Read Luke 15:1-24

In what ways have you experienced a relationship with a "lost one" in your family?

How might God be growing you through your relationship with him/her?

What disciplines may God be asking you to incorporate to deepen the tilt of your heart towards Him?

Pray and ask the Lord to help you know Him better. Over the next few days, notice and record His answer to this prayer.

MY FATHER'S EYES

"It was the first time I realized my mother is a person."

Kayla and I had been chatting about our mother-daughter relationship. We enjoy a deep love, respect, and friendship which has had its share of bumps as I learned how to relate to a daughter becoming an adult, and she learned how to relate to a mom who wasn't always right.

Kayla recalled the day our adult-to-adult relationship began to change for the better. She was home from college. Neither of us remember the details, but she remembers I was upset, and she felt she had done nothing for which I should be upset. She recollected sitting on her bed thinking, "My mom is really angry with me, but she can't punish me. She can't take away the car I pay for or keep me from seeing friends she doesn't know when I go back to the dorm room she doesn't live at. And, I haven't done anything. Ohhhh, my mom isn't mad. She's hurt!"

In that moment, Kayla saw me as more than a woman with parental authority in her life; someone she didn't want to disappoint but with whom she had to assert her autonomy. She saw me as a person; a person with flaws, who is sometimes hurt, and acted accordingly. Her perspective changed. Consequently, her reactions changed. Seeing me as a person with feelings, helped her find empathy and compassion for a mom who was learning a new way to interact with her as an adult daughter. Her new perspective helped us both as we grew.

POINT OF VIEW

There is an interval between the twilight of youth and the sunrise of decrepitude which we call middle age. For me, it is a moratorium on self-delusion. When I turned 40, I felt more at ease with myself than at any other time in my life. I described my 40's as being old enough to know what to do and young enough to still enjoy doing it. I believed that until my late 40's when my body parts began forecasting imminent decline. Suddenly my knees were creating sound effects when I took the stairs and I needed three good rocks to get off the couch. I once maniacally searched for my phone while holding it in my hand!

For the most part, I enthusiastically embrace getting older, becoming a fully grown version of myself. I enjoyed my 40's and I am loving my 50's. If my 40's were freeing, my 50's have been fantabulous! However, along the way, I have had to come to terms with an inconvenient truth: young at heart does not equal young in body.

I am very nearsighted and need glasses for most anything except reading. When it's time for me to update my prescription, I usually purchase 2 pairs of glasses with transitional lenses and a pair of sunglasses. Transitional lenses darken in sunlight and lighten when indoors. I'm so used to them; I hardly notice the changes.

I arrived at the home of a dear friend for an afternoon gab fest. We sat chatting, and laughing at her kitchen island. My chatter slowed as something else drew my attention. I looked around her kitchen. It was dark. Too dark for 1:00 p.m. on a sunny summer day. I checked her morning room, her great room, looked up at the lights in the ceiling. Everywhere was dim. What in the world could be wrong?

Did she have a brown out? Maybe she burned something and there was lingering smoke in the air. I scratched my head trying to figure out what was wrong. Finally, I reached up and pulled off my glasses to clean them. Suddenly, the world around me brightened. Cue the chorus!

Contrary to what I thought, the problem was mine, not hers. I did not have on my glasses with the transition lenses. I had mistakenly put on my sunglasses with the prescription lenses and kept them on, never noticing that the lens did not lighten. I shook my head, put on my regular glasses and all was right as rain.

My friend and I laughed at my premenopausal-brain moment in her kitchen. Later, I thought about my initial reaction. I had blamed my friend for my inability to see clearly. How arrogant was that? My vision was skewed but somehow it was her fault. She had a power issue in her home. She burned something in her home. My mistake. My glasses. Her fault. Not once during the time I ticked off possible reasons for the darkness in her home did it occur to me to check my own glasses.

OFF BY AN INCH, OFF BY A MILE

Perspective, the way we see something, the interpretation of information in relationship to ourselves, is shaped by the experiences, values, states of mind, belief systems, and assumptions which we bring into each and every situation. We use all of that to filter and assess facts. Our assessment then informs our reality, which then dictates how we act or react. The importance of perspective cannot be stressed enough. A skewed perspective isn't always as comical as my incident with the glasses, nor as easily resolved. Not only can it keep us oblivious to blind spots, but it can also strain relationships. If we aren't using objective filters based on truth, our lives and relationships will become unstable.

> Sometime later Paul said to Barnabas, "Let us go back and visit the believers in all the towns where we preached the word of the Lord and see how they are doing." Barnabas wanted to take John, also called Mark, with them, but Paul did not think it wise to take him, because he had deserted them in Pamphylia and had not continued with them in the work. They

*had such a sharp disagreement that they parted company.
Barnabas took Mark and sailed for Cyprus, but Paul chose
Silas and left, commended by the believers to the grace of the
Lord. He went through Syria and Cilicia, strengthening the
churches.*
Acts 15:36-41

Paul and Barnabas were close friends and brothers-in-arms. Barnabas was Paul's mentor. Together, they preached the gospel all across the region. Paul was ready to go back to the people to whom they had ministered, for a wellness check. In the verses above, they were preparing for their second missionary journey. Barnabas wanted John Mark to go with them. Paul vehemently objected.

Paul had lost confidence in Mark because he had abandoned them during a leg of the previous journey in order to return to Jerusalem (Acts 13:13). Paul refused to place trust in someone he perceived as unreliable. Barnabas, who was also on that first journey, had a different perspective. Barnabas and Mark were cousins; they had a familial bond (Colossians 4:10). However, I don't believe that would be a valid enough reason for Barnabas' willingness to go on a second missionary journey with Mark. Something weightier than family love caused Barnabas to defend Mark to the point of separating from Paul. I think he looked at Mark and saw what the Father thought of him. I believe he saw Mark's heart for Christ, and his love for believers, and wanted to encourage his growth. Much like Julia did with her stepson, Liam.

"Honey, something is going on beyond what we can see."

Julia laid her hand on her husband's arm to catch his attention. Every time they tried to talk to Liam, their 13-year-old son, he crumbled. With the slightest correction or raise in volume, he tightened, and tears formed in his eyes. He could not respond to direct questions. Nathan, Julia's husband, was frustrated. Julia asked the Lord to help her see Liam as He does. Where Nathan saw disrespect, and defiance, Julia saw a need for attention and opportunities to build a relationship.

NONE UNSEEN

Both Matthew and Mark record an encounter Jesus had with a rich young man who wanted to follow Jesus; the Bible calls him a ruler. Mark, however, records a detail to which I'd like to draw your attention.

> As Jesus started on his way, a man ran up to him and fell on his knees before him. "Good teacher," he asked, "what must I do to inherit eternal life?" "Why do you call me good?" Jesus answered. "No one is good— except God alone. You know the commandments: 'You shall not murder, you shall not commit adultery, you shall not steal, you shall not give false testimony, you shall not defraud, honor your father and mother.'"
> "Teacher," he declared, "all these I have kept since I was a boy." Jesus looked at him and loved him. "One thing you lack," he said. "Go, sell everything you have and give to the poor, and you will have treasure in heaven. Then come, follow me." At this the man's face fell. He went away sad, because he had great wealth.
> Mark 10:17-22

Mark was so captivated by the thought of undisguised love on the face of Jesus, he made note of it as he listened to Peter's preaching. Jesus did more than answer the young man and turn his response into a teaching opportunity. He looked at the man with interest and understanding. Having looked, He saw him, and having seen, He loved him. Having loved him, He knew him. Jesus understood what was lodged in the young man's heart. He knew that wealth was the true god of the young man's life. He saw the young man's need, and offered him the solution; knowing the young man would turn away. Jesus looks and loves.

Jesus looks at and loves you. He looks at your family and loves them. Yours are the eyes He is using to expose your family to His deep compassion. Yours are the eyes the Father will use to notice the deep needs of your family members.

This truth was etched on my heart, on ordinary Saturday in a park.

My friend pastored a church that was having a picnic and outdoor service in the park across from their building. As I was at home determining what I was going to do first, the Holy Spirit began prodding. "Go to the picnic." I had no intention of going to the park that day. It was my birthday weekend. I had other plans. I could not ignore the Lord's prompting. All other plans were scuttled, and I drove to the park.

I was ready to go within 15 minutes of my arrival. I really did not want to be in the park. I was there strictly out of obedience to the Lord: kicking and screaming my way to conformity, nearly resentful of having plans interrupted. Sometimes it's really ugly in my heart. I stood there watching children play, listening to the choir sing, thinking, "Can I go, now?" Then my eyes scanned the gathered crowd and fell on a short, middle-aged, Caucasian woman enjoying the choir. The Lord directed me towards her. As I walked towards her, the Holy Spirit whispered in my heart, "She is a lesbian." I approached her, smiled, and asked if she was enjoying the choir. As we chatted, I began sharing the gospel of Jesus Christ.

"I am Jewish."

She wasn't saying that as an objection to our conversation, more as a point of possible contention for me as evidenced by her response to my next statement.

"Isn't that interesting. So was Jesus."

"Well, I am also a lesbian. Don't you people hate people like me?"

"Absolutely not. Let me tell you more about the God who loves us so much, He sent His son to rescue us from the penalty and power of sin."

We talked more. She did not come to know the Lord that day, but seeds were planted. She graciously accepted the offer of a bible, and she waited the five or so minutes it took for me to locate one in the church across the street.

I was sure I had accomplished God's plan for my day and prepared to leave. As I walked towards the parking lot, I saw an older, clearly homeless, Caucasian man leaning against a tree. The Lord redirected me
.

"Sir, how are you today? I'm Cheryl. What's your name?"

I extended my hand in greeting. He responded,

"Ma'am, my hands are too dirty for you to shake."

"Sir, it would honor me to shake your hand."

I went on to share the love of God with him. Now, surely, there could be no further reason for me to stay, so I prepared to leave.

As I walked towards the parking lot, I saw a Caucasian young man, about 19 years old, dressed in all black, eyeliner rimmed his eyes, black bracelets with long spikes encircled his wrist. They were nothing compared to the triceratops-like spiked formation of his moussed hair. By the time I reached him we were joined by my friend, the pastor of the church.

We learned the young man was, himself, the son of a pastor. He told us he would not be allowed in his father's church dressed as he was. We encouraged him to visit my friend's church and shared God's love with him as well. I prepared to leave. I bid goodbye to some friends and headed towards my car.

As I walked, I heard the Holy Spirit impress an order in my heart:

"Stop!"

I came to an immediate halt.

"You are missing it. I sent you to a middle-aged, Jewish, lesbian, an old homeless man, and a young punked-out kid. These are people My people traditionally reject. These are people I will send you to if you let Me. You will never look into the eyes of someone whom I do not love nor for whom Christ did not die!"

I was an African American, heterosexual, duly employed, woman of 30-something at the time. The Lord deliberately turned my attention to people who were as different from me as a cat is from a horse. I am so grateful for that day in the park. No matter how different or unreachable a person may seem to me, no one is unseen by the Father. No one is unloved by God. Not John Mark, 2000 years ago. Not those people in the park many years ago. Not Liam 10 years ago. Not your stepchildren today.

As we cease viewing our bonus children through the dimming lens of judgement, God's love for them takes shape in our hearts. Then we will obtain access to their hearts, along with opportunities to plant and water the Word of God, and bear fruit in our families.

THE UNFAIREST OF ALL

"I don't think the answer is continued punishment. We're not being effective."

Julia and Nathan had tried all they could think of to break through to Liam. Counseling. Talking. Yelling. Punishment. Then they gave it up to the Lord and the solution crystallized.

"Julia, would you mind if once a week, during the weekend, I take him out, just the two of us? We can do something we both enjoy, and it won't be for any reason other than spending time with him. No talking about anything heavy or important unless he wants to. Just time. I know it messes up our weekly..."

Julia shushed her husband. Her answering smile shone brighter than Times Square on New Year's Eve.

"Honey," she interrupted, "I think that's it! That's the God answer we need."

Two years of consistent, one-on-one, time with his father, having fun, talking about nothing, yet saying everything, reached Liam like nothing else could. It was not always easy. Adjustments needed to be made along the way on everyone's part. Julia wisely encouraged and relished in the retelling of their weekly father/son adventures, though she struggled with feeling excluded at times. Nathan listened more than he spoke though he wrestled with impatience at Liam's slow progress.

Eventually Liam let them in again. He received correction in the loving spirit in which it was given. He received love. He gave it as well. They did not treat Liam according to his actions. They treated him in accord with their desire to see him free of the turmoil which caused him to shut down or behave badly. They allowed consequences, gave appropriate discipline, but always affirmed and loved him. The Holy Spirit directed them to treat Liam like the Father treats us.

God is absolutely not fair. He is good to people who hate Him. He allows bad things to happen to people who love Him. Want and disease occur in the lives of people who praise Him. Healing and prosperity occur in the lives of people who do not acknowledge Him. He is the unfairest of all, and I, for one, am thankful He is.

The Psalmist wrote in Psalm 103:

> *"The Lord is compassionate and gracious, slow to anger, abounding in love. He will not always accuse, nor will He harbor His anger forever; He does not treat us as our sins deserve or repay us according to our iniquities."* (v. 8-10)

Jeremiah wrote in Lamentations:

> *"Yet this I call to mind and therefore I have hope: Because of the Lord's great love we are not consumed, for His compassion never fails. They are new every morning; great is your faithfulness."* (v. 21-23)

And Ezra wrote in his namesake book:

> *"What has happened to us is a result of our evil deeds and our great guilt, and yet, our God, you have punished us less than our sins deserved and have given us a remnant like this."* (Ezra 9:13)

God does not treat us according to what is warranted, but in accord with His character. His mercy exceeds His judgment. If He treated us according to our guilt, none of us would be able to endure the unrelenting, just punishment. Natural consequences are often mitigated by His love and mercy. He generously gives what we cannot earn. He lovingly withholds what is deserved. The difficulties He allows serve our good and His glory. Julia and Nathan discovered a bigger purpose in their struggles with Liam. A purpose which brought unexpected blessing and fruit to their marriage. Working through their family challenges together forged a deeper intimacy in their marriage.

MUST HAVES

Do you know that God loves us too much to be primarily concerned with our happiness? We have an abundantly rich life in Jesus Christ, and the promise of an exponentially better eternal life to come. However, undisturbed happiness on this side of Heaven is not part of the deal. Joy, peace, wholeness, Christlikeness, victory, goodness, acceptance, love, yes! Happiness, not so much. We are loved too much for our fulfillment in life to rest on something as circumstantial as happiness.

As a young Christian, I believed life would turn out the way I wanted to I just "said so." If I faced difficulties surely God would rescue me, and quickly, so I would not have to endure anything too challenging. Except He didn't, and I did. As I matured, I discovered that any brokenness in my world, whether brought on by my choices, the choices of others, or life, were tools through which God glorified Himself and perfected His daughter.

God, who has the ability to intervene and keep painful situations from touching our lives, doesn't always act to shield us from pain. However, He always acts in the most loving and beneficial ways. He uses the hurt, challenges, and disappointments that come as a result of living in a fallen world, to display His goodness, purify our character and mold us into His image.

God is at work in the complications of your family. Moreover, He employs the complications for your good. They work for Him to help you. You will find the difficulties you walk through with your children will bring great blessing. God uses the challenges to:

Refine us:

> See, I have refined you, though not as silver; I have tested you in the furnace of affliction. For my own sake, for my own sake,

I do this. How can I let myself be defamed? I will not yield my glory to another. Isaiah 48:10-11

I frequently asked God for a specific physical healing in my life. He is able but thus far, He has chosen that it is better for me to live with this affliction. If it were better for me, and more glorifying to Him, He would heal me. My brokenness serves the King. Our afflictions are used to clarify God's image; to amplify His glory, the weightiness of His presence, in our lives.

Humble us:

> *He humbled you, causing you to hunger and then feeding you with manna, which neither you nor your ancestors had known, to teach you that man does not live on bread alone but on every word that comes from the mouth of the Lord.*
> *Deuteronomy 8:2-3*

God uses difficulties to strip us of self-sufficiency. We are ill-equipped to carry the weight of life. I know we like to think we can, but independence is a road to frustration and destruction. God lovingly allows circumstances in our life to drive us to seek and turn to Him for help. It creates in us a greater dependency on the One who is able to carry the weight of life and lead us to overcoming. Our blended family dynamics are exactly what we need to keep us dependent on the Lord.

Focus us:

> *Therefore, we do not lose heart. Though outwardly we are wasting away, yet inwardly we are being renewed day by day. For our light and momentary troubles are achieving for us an eternal glory that far outweighs them all. So, we fix our eyes not on what is seen, but on what is unseen, since what is seen is temporary, but what is unseen is eternal. 2*
> *Corinthians 4:16-18*

I had spent the morning of the day we received my cancer diagnosis in worship, intending to read Psalm 23. I stopped at the first half of the first verse, "The Lord is my Shepherd..." Suddenly, my heart was captivated by the majesty and greatness of the Lord who took care of me. I worshipped. Later, after the doctor called us, I went back to the room where I have morning devotion and sat in silence. Eventually I asked, "Well, Papa. They say I have cancer. What are we going to do about that?" I waited in the silence. A question bubbled up in my heart, "What's changed?"

The first verse of Psalm 23 came rushing back to my mind. Nothing had changed! The majestic, sovereign Lord was still at the helm of my life. I remember the joy and lightness that touched my heart. I prayed, "Father, whether I live or die, let me walk through this in a way which glorifies Your Name." We live in a temporal world. A fading "shadowland" to quote C.S. Lewis. Yet, we live for an eternal King. Challenges help us relinquish our hold on the temporal so we can focus on the eternal.

Assign us:

> *Praise be to the God and Father of our Lord Jesus Christ, the Father of compassion and the God of all comfort, who comforts us in all our troubles, so that we can comfort those in any trouble with the comfort we ourselves receive from God. 2 Corinthians 1:3-4*

Before the ink was dry on the divorce decree from my first marriage, I began meeting hurting women everywhere. Strange women would start talking to me about challenges in their marriages. Friends were sending women to me. God comforted me through the divorce, then sent women to me who were facing the same struggles. He comforts and leads us through pain with others in mind. Thus, at the right time, we are able to empathize and comfort them with what we received from God. Oh, how He loves us!

We ask God to remove affliction because it's painful and hard, but affliction is a tool of transformation. God uses pressure to form diamonds, irritants to form pearls, and dissolves the caterpillar to form a butterfly. The in between is messy. Rough. Transformation is not a pleasure trip. I remember once waxing poetic about the grand process of a caterpillar becoming a butterfly. Then I found out what actually happens to the caterpillar in the cocoon.

The gorgeous, admirable, blue morpho that emerges from the cocoon is born of a disgusting transaction. The caterpillar secures itself inside a cocoon, then begins to digest itself, releasing enzymes to dissolve all of its tissue. Yuck! The infrastructure for transformation, called imaginal discs, survives the digestive process. Once the caterpillar has disintegrated all of its tissue, except the imaginal discs, those discs use the protein in the caterpillar soup to fuel the cell division needed to form its adult features. Everything the caterpillar needs to become a butterfly is already in the caterpillar but "what was" has to die in order to make room for the beauty we enjoy.

Julia, Nate, and Liam had everything they needed to become a bonded blended family, but they also needed the pressure of the challenges they faced to reveal the treasure and beauty within.

EYES THAT SET US FREE

At the end of his life, with only Luke by his side, Paul asked Timothy to bring Mark to him because Mark was helpful to him in his ministry (2 Timothy 4:11). The same Mark which Paul stubbornly refused to take on his second missionary journey. I believe God used Barnabas to encourage Mark. Barnabas saw beyond the challenges and hurt caused by Mark's actions and Mark was freed to grow more fully into the faithfulness. I believe Paul's rejection of Mark was also part of God's growth plan for Mark. At some point, Paul and Mark reconciled. When Paul needed someone to help him continue his work while he waited for his execution, it was Mark he wanted.

I will not attempt to detail all God says about who we are in Christ. Even the bible does not reveal everything:

> Dear friends, now we are children of God, and what we will be has not yet been made known. But we know that when Christ appears, we shall be like him, for we shall see him as he is. 1 John 3:2

If chosen, redeemed, accepted, perfected, loved, whole, freed, delightful, heir, royal, priest, holy, aromatic, kept, and protected, aren't enough to thrill you, there is more to come! We don't even know all that we are because all that we are will not be fully revealed until Christ appears. There is more to us than meets the eye. There is more to our bonus children as well.

The stepmom who bears fruit, lives from God's perspective. For her, struggles in her relationship with her stepchildren provide opportunities to lean, pray, hope, and rejoice. The children causing her grief are people to love rather than problems to be managed. Hurting hearts are conditions in which the miraculous, redeeming power of God can work. Don't be disappointed by the imperfections of your stepchildren. The God who looks at you without condemnation empowers you to look at your stepchildren in the same way. View your family with eyes full of faith. Wait on the Lord and be of good courage.

TREASURE HUNT

Alright sisters, it's time to go on a little adventure. Grab your tools, namely your bible, journal, and pen, and let's do a little digging. Take an "inventory" of your bonus children. What glimpses of God's fingerprint do you see in their lives?

◊   Natural gifts and talents
◊   Activities which bring them joy
◊   Ways in which they show love, and kindness

How might you encourage their gifts, show an interest in them? (Sign up for a class with them. Learn about the activity. Surprise them with homemade chemistry experiments if they're good at science. Get creative.)

What issues or challenges are dampening the impact of those things you inventoried?

Pray for them. Ask the Lord to help you see them as He does. Ask Him to keep you aware of opportunities for encouragement and planting seeds. Ask Him to teach you how to speak life over them. Ask the Lord to strengthen them to overcome their challenges, and to heal them from emotional pain.

SAFE SHEPHERDS

My stepdaughter entered our bedroom around 2:30 a.m. She tip-toed to my side of the bed and tapped my arm. By the time I was fully awake, she was back at the door waiting for me.

"Cheryl, can I talk to you?"

This was not an unusual scene. The time might have been on the early side, or late depending on your perspective, but there was nothing unusual about her wanting to talk with me. In fact, all my girls, my bio-daughter, and both bonus daughters, seek me out.

I interviewed each kid individually for the Stepmom Sanity podcast. At some point, during the interviews with the daughters (bio and step), they each mentioned some variation of the same theme:

"I feel safe with you."

I don't know when I made the decision. However, I can say with certainty, only heavy dependence on the Lord helped me fulfill the promise I made to the unborn daughter I carried many years ago: "I will always be a safe place for you." When I became a stepmom, that promise extended to include all my kids, to the degree they would accept it.

The Bible tells us over and over again, God is our place of safety. Psalm 91:2 is one of nearly 70 I found (and I am probably missing a few): *I will say of the Lord, "He is my refuge and my fortress, my God, in whom I trust."*

God is our refuge, our sanctuary and hiding place. You and I have recourse for relief in God. We can trust Him with our most authentic selves. He sees it all and welcomes us still. He lovingly shows us Mommas how to hold sacred space in which our children experience His grace and mercy. He teaches us to shepherd: to lead, guide, love, and minister. He teaches us to shelter: to create a refuge where they are at ease, transparent, and accepted.

HEART OF THE SHEPHERD

I came awake as I sat straight up from a sound sleep. This would not be noteworthy except for the fact this happened the morning of my first day home after the full hysterectomy I underwent to remove cancer. I was not supposed to be able to sit up that quickly or at all. Not without any pain. I had no pain.

According to my surgeon, I needed medication in order to manage the pain. I refused to take the prescribed narcotics. The other option was to take alternating doses of Tylenol and Ibuprofen at specific intervals over a 24-hour period. I had a dose of one scheduled at 3:00 a.m. and a dose of another scheduled at 5:00 a.m., which meant I needed to set my alarm. On the night in question, the alarm went off and Jonathan woke up to help me for the 3:00 a.m. dose. We went back to sleep to get a few minutes of much needed rest before my next dose. I began dreaming.

In the dream, I was in bed in my dark bedroom. A doctor stood at the end of my bed chatting with me about the surgery. Suddenly the doctor disappeared. An orderly, dressed in white, was standing next to my bed. He held out his hands, as if to assist me, and said, "Come on. It's time to take your medicine." It was at that moment I awoke and sat up. The dream was so real I looked over at Jonathan to see if he had helped me up. He was sound asleep.

I reached for my phone. It was 5:05 a.m. I had forgotten to set the alarm for the 5:00 a.m. dose of pain meds! Whether the Lord sent the dream or allowed the brain He created to store, organize, and recall a set of data which caused the dream is immaterial. I had a dream which woke me at the exact moment I needed to take a dose of medicine, and I sat up without pain when I should not have been able to. The Lord takes care of His people.

Jesus is the Good Shepherd. The One who was, is and is to come.

Foretold in the book of Isaiah: *Like a shepherd He will tend His flock, In His arm He will gather the lambs and carry them in His bosom; He will gently lead the nursing ewes. Isaiah 40:11*

Revealed in the Gospel of John: *"I am the good shepherd; I know my sheep and my sheep know me, just as the Father knows me and I know the Father, and I lay down my life for the sheep." John 10:14-15*

Anticipated in Revelation: *For the Lamb at the center of the throne will be their shepherd; He will lead them to springs of living water. And God will wipe away every tear from their eyes. Revelation 7:17*

Throughout scripture, God uses the function of shepherding and the character of the shepherd to illustrate the relationship the Lord Jesus Christ has with those called to God through Him. Those scriptures paint an arresting portrait of a King whose attention and individual care of each of His sheep is precise and devoted. Jesus has pledged Himself to you and me. He has pledged Himself to our care.

His shepherding provides:
◊ Intimacy and Belonging (John 10:14-15)
◊ Protection (Psalm 23:4)
◊ Specificity (John 10:16)
◊ Healing (Psalm 23:5)
◊ Recovery (Luke 15:4)
◊ Provision (Psalm 23:2)
◊ Respite and Rest (Revelations 7:17)
◊ Safety and Shelter (John 10:28-29)
◊ Sacrificial Love (John 10:11)

◊   Reward (1 Peter 5:4)

As recipients of our Shepherd's care, you and I are called to shepherd in our family.

A SHEPHERD CALLED, "YOU"

My friend Summer emphasizes the shepherding role of stepmoms, writing: "We are called to share God's love and show His love to everyone in our flock...we shepherd others to Christ...we receive grace upon grace. We receive it as His lost sheep and offer it to others in our flock."
Peter wrote in his first letter:

> To the elders among you, I appeal as a fellow elder and a witness of Christ's sufferings who also will share in the glory to be revealed: Be shepherds of God's flock that is under your care, watching over them—not because you must, but because you are willing, as God wants you to be; not pursuing dishonest gain, but eager to serve; not lording it over those entrusted to you, but being examples to the flock. And when the Chief Shepherd appears, you will receive the crown of glory that will never fade away. 1 Peter 5:1-4

Friend, you may not be an elder in a church body, but you are an elder in your home. As a mom in your home, you are part of the Chief Shepherd's team. You have been called to your family to lead, guide, care for, and protect the children entrusted to you by God. For however long, and at whatever interval, they are in your care.

To mother children not biologically your own is not an occurrence of happenstance. The Good Shepherd led you. He ordered your steps so that you would show up in your family. Now show up in your family. Care for them as the Father cares for you. Place your hand in the strong grip of Jesus and trust Him to lead in your stepmomming. He has equipped you to shelter and shepherd.

STORM SHEPHERDS

None of this is easy. There are too many complicated subsets for easy. We have family, extended family, and sub-family groups to manage; bio-parents to bio-kids, stepparents to step-kids, bio-kids to stepchildren, step and bio grandparents, aunts, uncles and cousins, and so on. Throw in the normal ebb and flow of life and it's enough to make you wanna holler. Yet, God has called you to it. He is with you in it. He specializes in the seemingly impossible.

My stepdaughter and I sat on her bed that early morning and chatted. As she spoke, I vacillated between anger at the person who put her in the predicament she faced, and desire to remain the stable presence she needed. That early morning was the opening salvo in what became a four-year trial as my stepdaughter worked to extricate herself and recover from a toxic relationship.

Mark records a remarkable encounter the disciples had with Jesus. He had been in a boat on the lake, teaching a large crowd, and was ready to take the disciples for a little rest. Jesus requested they go to the other side (Mark 4). Several boats travelled with them. Jesus went to sleep in His boat. A storm arose. The NIV calls it a furious squall. It was a great windstorm which caused waves to overtake the boat. Jesus slept. The wind did not wake Him. The water filling the boat did not wake Him. The disciples woke Him with complaints, "Don't you care that we're going to die?" Jesus stood, calmly rebuked the winds and waves and asked, "Why are you so afraid? Do you still have no faith?"

Turmoil arrives in our lives, and the lives of our children, with regularity. The Lord is quite aware of the storms we face. Often, He has deliberately set us on a path to intersect with a storm. Despite the ferocity of the wind, and the threat of submersion, Jesus remains calm, unthreatened, and unbothered. He is seated in heavenly places and adjudicates all our days from a seat ensconced in peace. We are seated with Him in Heavenly places. Positionally secure. Positionally victorious. Despite what is going on around us. Why allow the din of inner turmoil to rise to the level of the noise of external turmoil?

Jesus is our shepherd in the storm. Our ballast when life is dicey. Familiarity with the safety we have in Christ is our key to maintaining peace. We know at any moment He can silence the howling wind and restrain the billowing sea. Because He is with us, we are safe even if He chooses not to act immediately. In Christ, you and I are perfectly situated to pull our children into the hiding place under the shadow of His wings. Sitting on the bed that morning I turned towards the Lord, who calms internal storms as effectively as He does storms on the sea. And, He helped me shepherd my bonus daughter in her own storm.

THE SHEPHERD'S ROD

"Honey, you have some tough decisions to make and I'm praying for you. Let's talk some of this through"

Ancient shepherds employed several tools in the execution of their trade; two of which were the rod and the staff. The staff was a long, thin, stick with a hook or crook at one end. The rod was a shorter, club-like tool used to fight off wild animals and direct the sheep.

Sheep are prone to stray because they are easily led. Unlike many other animals, they have no natural defenses. Good shepherds use the rod to prod the sheep in the direction of the shepherd's leading, defend the sheep against ravenous predators, or pull them out of dangerous situations.

Not everything Jesus says to us sounds loving, but everything He says is because of His relentless love for us. He commands us to forgive because offense traps us in soul-damaging unforgiveness and bitterness. He challenges us to consider ourselves less not to see us grovel, but because He stands in opposition to the proud while the humble are graced by Him. He commands us to love Him more than we love anyone or anything else, even our very own lives, because only in Him is true life found. The direction and commands given to us by Jesus are for our benefit.

It is the same with our own little flock. The Bible points out, in several places, that we are God's own flock (Psalm 23, 79:13, 95:7). In Isaiah and Jeremiah, the bible mentions our tendency to, like sheep, go astray, leave our resting place, and direct our own steps (Isaiah 53:6, Jeremiah 50:6). If the tendency to stray and self-direct is not curtailed, many of us would tumble headlong off a cliff. Shepherding very often requires redirection of wayward sheep for the benefit of the flock under our care.

I listened when our daughter needed to purge her feelings. There were also times I prodded. It was a struggle for the family to know how best to support her, but her heart was on the line. I could not afford to be a lazy shepherd. If some of the issues she wrestled with were allowed to go unchecked, it would have been a much harder road of recovery for her. At the Holy Spirit's leading I spoke truth to combat the lies she started believing. I did not enjoy watching her stew in the tension between truth and lies, but that was much better than watching her tumble off a cliff.

When I heard the tinge of bitterness in her voice, I redirected her to forgiveness. When she felt guilty for limiting or cutting off interaction, I offered respite with conversations about healthy boundaries. And when she had tough decisions to make, we prayed for wisdom and strength. I learned when to prod and when to allow her to rest. I learned how to refresh and how to protect without overwhelming her. I learned all of this by listening to and imitating my Good Shepherd.

We are disciples: followers, learners, leaners, beholders, and imitators of Christ. His Spirit lives in us, and empowers us to love as He loves, to see as He sees, to obey the Father as He obeys the Father, to do what Christ does. In this way we shepherd our stepchildren straight to the Chief Shepherd.

COME ON IN

However, none of that is possible without first gaining access and influence with our stepchildren. They will not grant access if they do not feel safe. They will not accept our guidance unless they know our care for them is pure, reliable, and resilient. The early morning talks, midnight prayers, revelations, tears, confessions, fun, and connection would not have happened with my daughter or my bonus children without them first feeling safe. For my daughter, safety was the natural state of a daughter loved and cared for by her mother all her life. For my stepchildren, it was a process.

They did not know me. They weren't sure I could be trusted. They were uncertain if I were an addition to their lives or a thief, robbing them of their father's time and affection. As far as they were concerned, I had some proving to do. There were times I hated the skepticism, but I understood. As I prayed and leaned on Jesus, He moved me beyond resentment, helped me adjust my thinking and focus, and taught me how to be a safe stepmom.

A safe stepmom provides comfort, guidance, wisdom, and protection without deliberately threatening bio mom's role. Her identity is moored in Christ's love therefore, she need not pressure her family for affirmation. A safe stepmom is a woman whose security is established in the stalwart Sovereignty of God. She is free to be safe because she is free in Christ. She:

◊   Accepts her children without trying to change them.
◊   Is responsive to their feelings without taking them personally.
◊   Listens and hears what is being said. (James 1:19)

◊   Is humble enough to admit when she is wrong.

◊   Leans on the Spirit to restore (Galatians 6:1-2)

◊   Is focused on pointing them to Christ, not drawing them to herself

◊   Keeps confidences (Proverbs 11:13)

◊   Is available and present

◊   Provides a judgement free zone

◊   Is honest, even when the truth is painful (Colossians 3:9-10)

◊   Speaks the truth in love and grace (Colossians 4:6)

◊   Takes responsibility for her own emotional health

◊   Relies on God's word for dispensing opinion and advice

◊   Recognizes the holy privilege of influencing the heart of someone God loves.

It is a tall order for a woman in a role in which she often finds herself isolated. It would be impossible to accomplish on our own. We can't. God can. I've said it before, I'll repeat it here: You and I do not have to stepmother in our own strength. The Holy Spirit wants to come alongside us and strengthen us for what God has called us to accomplish. God is at work in each of us. He has given us the desire and the ability to carry out His will. You, in Christ, are one of the pipelines He uses to envelope your children in His love, acceptance, and safety. He has enabled you to do it.

SHEPHERDED TOO

Last year, I started feeling a bit unappreciated by my children. There is an organic, unrefined, give and take of relationship with Kayla. We can chat, laugh, and solve world problems. With my bonus children, those types of conversations were generally initiated by me. Most of the conversations initiated by my bonus daughters were around an issue they faced.

They were not being deliberately hurtful at all. In their minds, I was the parent to turn to when they needed calm reassurance and prayer. It is a blessing to be thought of that way. It is also distressing to be only thought of that way.

The girls had stopped by for a visit. We sat in the family room talking about a few things they had been facing over the previous months. It was the perfect time, and the Holy Spirit gave me the words to say:

"Girls, I feel very honored that you all come to me when you are struggling with something. I really do. Sometimes though it can feel like I'm being used. I don't get the 'Hey, "how you doing" phone calls and that hurts."

They were silent for a moment. They listened, promised they would do better. A little while later they left. On Christmas day I received a beautiful gift and note from them. I won't share the details of what was written but I will say they heard me, they sheltered me, they cared for me in the specific way I needed.

Stepmoms who shepherd will often find themselves shepherded as well. The safe place you build for others is sacred space set aside for those you shepherd and for you. A space made where you can be yourself, connect on a deep level, and hear the truth about your own flaws without defensiveness because you know what is shared is encased in love. Safety given. Safety returned.

TREASURE HUNT

Alright sisters, it's time to go on a little adventure. Grab your tools, namely your bible, journal, and pen, and let's do a little digging.

Read Psalm 23 and the 10th Chapter of John.

What characteristics of the Good Shepherd speak to you?

How has God shown Himself to be a shepherd in your life?

In what ways may the Lord be challenging you to shepherd your family?

Ask the Holy Spirit to show you the importance of your ministry to your stepchildren.

THIS HEART IS ON FIRE

I sat to write this chapter and a worship song, I learned a long time ago, bubbled up in my heart:

In Your Presence,
In Your Presence there is peace.
In Your Presence,
In Your Presence there is joy.
I will linger, I will stay in Your Presence
Day by day, 'till your likeness may be seen in me.
Carried away, carried away, with my Lord,
Carried away, carried away, with my Lord.
I will linger, I will stay in Your Presence
Day by day, 'till your likeness may be seen in me.
Holy, holy, holy, holy is my Lord.
Holy, holy, holy, holy is my Lord.
I will linger, I will stay in Your Presence
Day by day, 'till your likeness may be seen in me.

I searched for the composer but could not find his or her name anywhere. I'd like to thank that person. This song is a simple depiction of a passionate pursuit of the Holy and desirable King.

The joy of my day is any time spent in the presence of the Lord. At any moment I can, and often do, turn my heart towards Him in adoration. I enjoy His presence as much in the mundane tasks of my day as I do in my set aside time of devotion. He is my deepest satisfaction.

God is the fulfillment of absolutely everything we could ever possibly need. There is nothing you require which He cannot supply. He is sufficient for any demand. He furnishes what is missing. Our lack becomes immaterial in light of His abundance.

The time we spend beholding Him makes Him bigger. Faith takes flight, confidence to obey Him soars. A glimpse of His glory, a touch from His hand, and suddenly we are fit, effective, and ready.

A SINGLE AIM

I read an article about soil erosion which included a picture of an 80ft high ironwood tree which is a shoreline tree prominent in Hawaii. The wide and tall tree had been situated on the beach for years. The picture arrested my attention because there was a good deal of soil erosion beneath the tree, yet it stood tall and erect. The ocean washed away enough sand that three feet of the tree's root system was exposed. However, the depths of the roots in the ground surpassed the height of the roots exposed. Soil erosion was no match for a stubborn tree with a single aim of driving deep.

Paul wrote to the Philippians:

> But whatever were gains to me I now consider loss for the sake of Christ. What is more, I consider everything a loss because of the surpassing worth of knowing Christ Jesus my Lord, for whose sake I have lost all things. I consider them garbage, that I may gain Christ and be found in him, not having a righteousness of my own that comes from the law, but that which is through faith in Christ the righteousness that comes from God on the basis of faith. I want to know Christ yes, to know the power of his resurrection and participation in his sufferings, becoming like him in his death, and so, somehow, attaining to the resurrection from the dead.
> Philippians 3:7-11

There is nothing compared to knowing Jesus. There is no accomplishment that compares to the thrill of knowing Jesus is our savior, Lord, and friend. There is a quote attributed to St. Augustine, but Raphael Simon actually said it: "To fall in love with God is the greatest of all romances; To seek Him, the greatest adventure; To find him, the greatest human achievement."

If I won a Pulitzer, befriended the President, and built a home in Fiji, it would be as worthless as yesterday's trash compared to the value of intimacy with Christ. Every attainment is an opportunity to praise Him. Every distress, an opportunity to lean on Him.

Knowing Him has become the dominant intention of my life. My stubborn focus is an intimate relationship with the God who loves me. Being unwanted hurts; you feel raw and exposed. However, like the tree existing in eroded soil, exposure is no match for a woman with the single aim of driving deep into knowing God. Those raw feelings yield to the joy of knowing Him.

God bids us to know, and enjoy knowing, Him. He wants us to notice who He is; taste and see that He is good. Author John Piper wrote: "But to enjoy him we must know him. Seeing is savoring. If he remains a blurry, vague fog, we may be intrigued for a season. But we will not be stunned with joy, as when the fog clears and you find yourself on the brink of some vast precipice," (John Piper, *Desiring God: Meditations of a Christian Hedonist*).

His visage stuns with joy. It is intoxicating. He is altogether lovely. He is full of majesty and glory. Light and truth are His garments and everlasting are His ways. He is nothing but good and everything that is good comes from Him. The more we seek God, the more we know Him. The more we know Him, the more we want to know Him. The more we want to know Him, the more we seek Him. Such a delightful circle.

What do you know of Him? Do you know Him as the lover of your soul, the One who soothes, restores, protects and comforts? Is He the provider of all your needs? He loves lavishly and sacrificially. His goodness surrounds us. His glory is our rear guard. He is more wonderful than I could ever express! I am overcome by the greatness of our Mighty God.

God longs for us to know the security of living in deep devotion to Him to see and believe He is who He says He is. A vibrant awareness that God is with us and His Spirit is working in and through us is our anchor for everyday life, whether that life is messy and complicated or harmonious and easy.

GIVING GOOD GIFTS

I watched my husband as he chatted with my mother. He exudes intelligence, kindness, humor, and integrity. Oh, I love that man of mine! He was unaware of my observation. I was enthralled with him. Just an ordinary do-nothing day, but love swelled in my heart as he talked and laughed with my mother.

Let me tell you Sis, I don't always feel that way about my hubby. Sometimes we don't agree. Sometimes I need a moment before I can engage with him. He's a fixer. Sometimes I don't want to be fixed. On those days my gaze is not so loving. I'm more likely to roll my eyes than bat them. I've discovered an unexpected benefit to spending time with the Lord. The more consistent I am in my pursuit of God, the more I like my husband. I am less likely to be irritated by or impatient with my family when I've been in the sweet presence of my Savior.

One of the best gifts we can give our families is our personal, passionate, pursuit of God. Dr. Tony Evans wrote in his book, *The Power of Knowing God*, "When you are intimately close to God in such a way that your spirit moves in cadence with His own, you will grow in the wisdom you need for every choice you have to make." To become like Him, to shepherd like Him, trust in Him and love like Him while we wait, we must know God.

Knowing God isn't knowing scripture or liturgy or knowing Christian-speak. It isn't going to church or even praying. Knowing God is an experience which pierces to the depth of our souls. Knowing God is looking into the glory revealed in His word, then allowing that revelation to become our greatest reality.

Knowing God is finding our identity in belonging to Him. Knowing God is having a life defined by our relationship to and with God.

I have had occasion to read a letter ostensibly written by a pastor in Zimbabwe just before he was martyred. We don't know much about the preacher, but we can learn from his single-hearted devotion to the Lord. He writes:

> "I'm part of the fellowship of the unashamed. I have the Holy Spirit power. The die has been cast. I have stepped over the line. The decision has been made. I'm a disciple of his. I won't look back, let up, slow down, back away, or be still.

> "My past is redeemed, my present makes sense, my future is secure. I'm finished and done with low living, sight walking, smooth knees, colorless dreams, tamed visions, worldly talking, cheap giving, and dwarfed goals. I no longer need preeminence, prosperity, position, promotions, plaudits, or popularity. I don't have to be right, first, tops, recognized, praised, regarded, or rewarded.

> "I now live by faith, lean in his presence, walk by patience, am uplifted in prayer, and I labor with power. My face is set, my gait is fast, my goal is heaven, my road is narrow, my way is rough, my companions are few, my Guide reliable, my mission clear.

> "I cannot be bought, compromised, detoured, lured away, turned back, deluded, or delayed. I will not flinch in the face of sacrifice, hesitate in the presence of the enemy, pander at the pool of popularity, or meander in the maze of mediocrity. I won't give up, shut up, let up, until I have stayed up, stored up, prayed up, paid up, preached up for the cause of Christ.

> "I am a disciple of Jesus. I must go till he comes, give till I drop, preach till all know, and work till he stops me. And, when he

comes for his own, he will have no problem recognizing me . . .
my banner will be clear!"

The young pastor's entire life became defined by one identity, "I am a disciple of Jesus," an identity he refused to renounce. His determined stance, found in his papers after his death, has reached the hearts of millions across the world. We are blessed, spurred on, and ignited by his devotion.

We may not have the same reach as this letter, but we can have the same impact on the lives of those we do influence. The people in our immediate circle are the primary beneficiaries of hearts and attitudes softened and adjusted by time spent with the Lord. Our passionate pursuit of God is satisfaction for us and blessing for others.

JESUS AT THE CENTER

Kayla and I talk about relationships quite often. We scrutinize interpersonal patterns in all kinds of relationships (family, friendship, dating, and marriage), from every angle.

"Mom, how do you do it?"

"Do what, Kayla?"

"How do you forgive so easily? How do you stay so gracious?"

"I don't do it easily Kayla. The only way I can do anything is by the grace of God. Jesus makes all the difference and if it weren't for Him, your mother would be a hot mess!"

Dear one, step-mothering is ministry, service. Your ministry. My ministry. You and I have been perfectly positioned to make a God-sized difference in the lives of our stepchildren.

There are people in my life He wants to reach. There are people in your life He wants to reach. He has purposefully set you in your family, and me in mine, for the sake of our loved ones. However, there is no way you and I can glorify God in our stepparenting until it becomes Christ-centered.

Each of our children, at one time or another, have asked me to pray for them or one of their friends. Not only because they trust me, but because they know I trust Christ. They have seen Him work in our family and have heard us praising Him. Christ-centered step-mothering points our children to Christ as the source of hope, life, answers, and joy.

A Christ-centered stepmom relies on wisdom from above. There is no other god above our God. No one instructs Him. There is none to whom He answers. There is none who counsels Him, nor any to whom He must give an account. When He takes counsel, He counsels with Himself (Job 12:13). He is the source of true wisdom and understanding. "For the Lord gives wisdom; from his mouth come knowledge and understanding.," (Proverbs 2:6). The stepmom with her heart centered on Jesus, knows no greater authority than Jesus, Himself.

A Christ-centered stepmom is at rest because God is immutable. God will never change. We have confident trust and abiding hope because His character is sacrosanct. He is what He is and remains what He is consistently. "Every good and perfect gift is from above, coming down from the Father of the heavenly lights, who does not change like shifting shadows," (James 1:17). If He took care of you yesterday, you know He will take care of you today. If He soothed your hurt feelings and healed your wounded pride yesterday, He will do it today. The faithfulness of God blows ease and rest into our lives so that we can parent in peace.

Christ-centered stepmoms obey the Lord. The decisions and actions of Christ-centered stepmoms are evaluated based on how pleasing they are to the Lord. It doesn't matter if something is permissible, or "right". The heart of a stepmom focused on Jesus asks, "Is the decision I am about to make, the action I am preparing to take, are the words getting ready to come out of my mouth, pleasing to the Lord?" Paul wrote: Am I now trying to win the approval of human beings, or of God? Or am I trying to please people? If I were still trying to please people, I would not be a servant of Christ. (Galatians 1:10)

Christ-centered stepmoms rely on His strength. Nothing lays beyond Jesus' ability to change. The entire universe is upheld by the mere word of His power (Hebrews 1:3). He is fully able. He cannot be overthrown. No enemy can stand in His presence unless He allows it. Christ-centered stepmoms look to Him for the stamina, fortitude, and courage to love while waiting to be wanted. The bible tells us: I know that you can do all things, and that no purpose of yours can be thwarted (Job 42:2, ESV).

My beloved sister, I cannot begin to tell you how often I have failed at being a Christ-centered stepmom. There are moments the flesh is clearly in charge. You will stumble. You will sin. You will mess up.

We read in 1 John 1:8-10 : If we claim to be without sin, we deceive ourselves and the truth is not in us. If we confess our sins, he is faithful and just and will forgive us our sins and purify us from all unrighteousness. If we claim we have not sinned, we make him out to be a liar and his word is not in us.

Don't despair. The cross of Christ is a finished work. Jesus will restore you. Apologize to the person you offended. Repent to the Lord. Be restored to fellowship with Christ and your children. Christ-centered stepmoms are not sin-free, but they are fast confessors, who keep short accounts with the Lord.

The entire purpose of our lives is to bring praise and honor to God. It's time to remove yourself from the throne of your life, in every area. Give Jesus the lordship of your parenting. Let Him lead you.

STOKING FLAMES, DOUSING DISTRACTIONS

Endless errands, meetings, and doing, kept my tank empty. I had little time for "being." I was worn plumb dry. After a month of non-stop going, I noticed my relationships became strained and I was a bit closed off. I really enjoy listening to and praying with people. I am typically blessed by pointing them to a truth which God uses to bring healing or restoration. However, amid the rush, I no longer wanted to hear from people. I got irritated when people called. Finally, I cried out to God. His answer was an invitation to come away.

I have lived in homes with fireplaces for the last 30 years of my life. I've had gas fireplaces, electric fireplaces, and wood-burning fireplaces. By far, my favorite is wood burning. I love the smell of real logs burning, and the crackle of wood being consumed by the flames. Though, it's a lot of work. If you want to enjoy the fire for any length of time, you have to stoke the flame, and give the fire something on which to feed.

The Spirit of the Lord is always reaching for us; nudging us to pay attention, silence the noise, ignore the distractions, and tune in to His voice. He gives us the fuel to stoke the flames. We need only slow down, listen, then turn our attention towards the presence of the Lord, our true home.

The life we live can seem like an extended stay in Neverland; the dwelling of Peter Pan and the Lost Boys. Neverland's power over the children lost there was the ability to make them forget. Make them forget what it was like to have someone love and care for them, and that there was something far grander than their pretense.

Neverland kept the children distracted from what was real, good, and vibrant by feeding their appetites for play. Wendy saw through the illusion of Neverland and turned her attention towards home. Only she and her brothers made their way back.

The world has the ability to infiltrate with urgent needs, pressing deadlines, and endless cycles of chores, conflict, and competition, creating interference between us and the One who loves and cares for us. Worldly living keeps us distracted by feeding our appetite for vain ambition, material wealth, and indulgence. In the temporary appeasement of the flesh, we forget there is something far grander than this "neverland" in which we live. Only when we see through the illusion, and turn our attention towards home, are we able to break free from neverland's enchantment.

We are anointed by God to tear down strongholds in the lives of our families. We are called to prayerful parenting. We are placed to influence for the Kingdom of God. Neverland's distractions are dangerous to our mission. Our ardent pursuit of God affixes our heart on Christ above, from Whom comes our aid to stepmom well. The radiance of the Holy Spirit will burn brighter in our lives as we fan the flames of devotion to God.

My sister, I don't know what you are facing in your life and family. I don't know what needs are demanding your attention, or goals requiring pursuit. I don't know if you feel up to turning your attention towards your true home in Christ. Whether you are burning hot with devotion for God or barely holding on to faith, I want to encourage you to take steps towards stirring your passion and zeal for the Lord. Pray. Read His word. Share the gospel. Worship Him. Serve others. Get connected with people whose hearts are on fire as well. It will only better your life. Satisfaction, contentment, wisdom, and peace are the consequences of the pursuit of God. Consequences which bless you and those around you.

There are two quotes in decorative lettering on walls in my office. One is a declaration to the people who find themselves curled up in the oversized chair:

What we love most about our home is who we share it with.

The other is a reminder to do all for the glory of God:

Writing is my worship!

The offering of my writing is an outward expression of reverence for the One who gave me the talent.

Any role we assume in life could replace the word "writing;" Teaching is my worship. Singing is my worship. Taking care of the home I am blessed to live in is my worship. Intercession is my worship. Being a wife, a daughter, a sister, friend, mom. Being a stepmom is my worship. These are all vehicles through which we honor God.

Being a stepmom is ministry. Being a stepmom is worship. Being a stepmom is something else, too.

THE GOSPEL EMBODIED

Sandra unfurled the letter, sent to her for her birthday, from her bonus daughter, Crystal. The cherished letter was well creased from all of the folding and unfolding and discolored by a tear stain or two. Sandra's heart swelled with emotion and gratefulness yet again when she read:

*"You showed me how to live out my faith. I have watched you.
In every challenge you rock faith in Christ and I've seen His
goodness through you."*

For Sandra, there were no sweeter words Crystal could have written. Of all Sandra wanted for her children, bio and step, knowing God and believing in the One He sent, the Lord Jesus, is what she wanted most. It would thrill her to no end if God used her to lead them to Him. Being a stepmom is evangelism in action.

I am so very blessed to sit under the sound, biblical, teaching of Pastor Bob Shirock. He has a quote which I have placed in my memory vault:

"The gospel embraced is the gospel embodied."

To embody the Gospel is to become such a compelling representation of Jesus Christ, others are drawn to Him through you. No matter how well received, remembered, or recited, the real purpose of the Word of God, lies dormant until we see God the Word, Jesus Christ (John 1:1-3), on display in our lives. It is easy to say, "I live for the glory of God," but there is no power in that statement without corresponding demonstration.

Paul instructed Timothy:

"All Scripture is God-breathed and is useful for teaching,
rebuking, correcting and training in righteousness, so that the
servant of God may be thoroughly equipped for every good
work." 2 Timothy 3:16-17

Truth has an intended end. We engage the words we read, meditate on, listen to, or hear, on the pages of the bible. The words on the pages also engage us. They teach us about God. They rebuke and correct our wayward thinking. The bible instructs us how to live godly lives. It equips us to exhibit the power the gospel has to change a life. It trains us to imitate Christ:

"Follow God's example, therefore, as dearly loved children and
walk in the way of love, just as Christ loved us and gave
himself up for us as a fragrant offering and sacrifice to God."
Ephesians 5:1-2

To embody the gospel is to live like Christ lived, obey like Christ obeyed, reach like Christ reached, preach what Christ preached, love like Christ loved.

His love is welcoming, approachable, truthful, healing, present, and powerful. His love is given freely. That means, within you and me, lies the ability to be welcoming, honest, healing, present, and powerful towards our children. And to be all of that without any expectation of return.

Loving to get love is not love at all. It's emotional manipulation. To imitate Christ in our step-mothering is to give ourselves up to loving. Totally. Go all in. Walk in the way of love without reservation. His love. His is a love that approaches despite rejection, embraces without condemnation, confronts without destroying, gives before receiving.

You can love this way. It's in you because He's in you. There is nothing lacking in you. Your Heavenly Champion wants you to know: the wait is over. You are wanted. You are cherished. You are redeemed. You are justified. You are glorified. You are enabled. Embrace it. Open the Bible and read your covenantal reality. It's right there in black and white, all for you.

Trust God. He will help you forgive the slights. He will ease the pains, hush the heartache, and quench your thirst for family unity. He also cheers you on, equips you, loves you, and endorses you. Through good times and bad, He remains ever present, ever attentive, and ever empowering. So, love, my cherished sister. Love.

TREASURE HUNT

Alright sisters, it's time to go on a little adventure. Grab your tools, namely your bible, journal, and pen, and let's do a little digging.

How has your family benefited from you knowing God?

Read Ephesians 1:3-12
How does it make you feel to know you are already wanted?

Write out a prayer of thanksgiving praising God for choosing and sealing you.

POUR YOUR HEART

We are here, Sis. Where the rubber meets the road. You have decisions to make. Will you commit to serve your stepchildren even if they do not appreciate it? Will you love them even if they do not love you in return? Will you refresh when it is inconvenient? When you're tired?

Let's read Isaiah 58:10-11:

> ...and if you spend yourselves in behalf of the hungry
> and satisfy the needs of the oppressed,
> then your light will rise in the darkness,
> and your night will become like the noonday.
> The Lord will guide you always;
> he will satisfy your needs in a sun-scorched land
> and will strengthen your frame.
> You will be like a well-watered garden,
> like a spring whose waters never fail.

If you have answered the questions above with a resolved, "Yes" get ready to be spent, depleted, inconvenienced, and dried out. But know this; if you pour into your stepchildren and satisfy God's desire to love them through you, even as you find yourself in the desert, even while they are rejecting you, God will cause you to become a beacon to them. He, Himself, will strengthen you and satisfy your desires.

As you pour into your stepchildren, even when you feel tired, frustrated, and empty, God will fill you with His presence to keep you going. He will refill you with living water. You can pour because God furnishes a ceaseless supply of His Spirit.

I have listed a few scriptures to encourage generosity in loving your bonus children. Please take a moment to look over these scriptures. Pray over them. Memorize them and hide them in your heart. Ask questions of them. Ask God to open your understanding as you read. Most importantly, believe them and ask the Holy Spirit to help any unbelief.

These commandments that I give you today are to be on your hearts. Impress them on your children. Talk about them when you sit at home and when you walk along the road, when you lie down and when you get up. Deuteronomy 6:6-7

So in everything, do to others what you would have them do to you, for this sums up the Law and the Prophets. Matthew 7:12

A new command I give you: Love one another. As I have loved you, so you must love one another. By this everyone will know that you are my disciples, if you love one another. John 13:34-35

And hope does not put us to shame, because God's love has been poured out into our hearts through the Holy Spirit, who has been given to us. Romans 5:5

Be devoted to one another in love. Honor one another above yourselves. Romans 12:10

Let us therefore make every effort to do what leads to peace and to mutual edification. Romans 14:19

You, my brothers and sisters, were called to be free. But do not use your freedom to indulge the flesh; rather, serve one another humbly in love. Galatians 5:13

Do not let any unwholesome talk come out of your mouths, but only what is helpful for building others up according to their needs, that it may benefit those who listen. Ephesians 4:29

Be kind and compassionate to one another, forgiving each other, just as in Christ God forgave you. Ephesians 4:32

Not looking to your own interests but each of you to the interests of the others. Philippians 2:4

Therefore, as God's chosen people, holy and dearly loved, clothe yourselves with compassion, kindness, humility, gentleness and patience. Bear with each other and forgive one another if any of you has a grievance against someone. Forgive as the Lord forgave you. And over all these virtues put on love, which binds them all together in perfect unity. Colossians 3:12-14

Therefore encourage one another and build each other up, just as in fact you are doing. 1 Thessalonians 5:11

Above all, love each other deeply, because love covers over a multitude of sins. Offer hospitality to one another without grumbling. Each of you should use whatever gift you have received to serve others, as faithful stewards of God's grace in its various forms. 1 Peter 4:8-10

Be shepherds of God's flock that is under your care, watching over them—not because you must, but because you are willing, as God wants you to be; not pursuing dishonest gain, but eager to serve; not lording it over those entrusted to you, but being examples to the flock. 1 Peter 5:2-3

Dear children, let us not love with words or speech but with actions and in truth. 1 John 3:18

Dear friends, let us love one another, for love comes from God. Everyone who loves has been born of God and knows God. Whoever does not love does not know God, because God is love. This is how God showed his love among us: He sent his one and only Son into the world that we might live through him. This is love: not that we loved God, but that he loved us and sent his Son as an atoning sacrifice for our sins. 1 John 4:7-10

SECTION IV

Prayers for the Waiting Room

PRAYERS FOR THE WAITING ROOM

I pray hope has settled in your heart as you read the stories and reflected on the principles in this guide.

You will find a list of prayers written by a stepmom for stepmoms in this section. These may be repeated verbatim, but I encourage you to read through them first, then use them as prayer prompts. Allow the words and scriptures to invade your soul and elicit the real cries of your heart.

TO KNOW THE FATHER'S LOVE

If you were deprived of growing up in a loving, affirming environment. Or if your relationship experiences have left you wanting, you may believe you're incapable of loving well. This is a lie. All those who have become daughters (and sons) of the King through the shed blood of Jesus are translated into a family whose Father is not only loving but is Love Himself. He more than makes up for what we've missed.

Prayer

Heavenly Father, you are the Great God who works wonders and is covered in majesty. Yet, you direct Your goodness towards me and love me beyond my understanding. Your love for me is tender and ferocious, passionate and lavish, unconditional and sacrificial. It never runs out. I cannot exhaust it. I did not earn it. And I cannot lose it. Ever. I am redeemed and secure because of Your great love. I belong to You because You loved me and chose me even before You created the Earth. Help me to be rooted and grounded in Your love for me and not expect others to meet emotional needs only You can meet. Help me to understand how immeasurable your love is for me. Help me to notice, experience, and worship You when You demonstrate Your love for me in small and big ways. I thank You for answering this prayer, and I stand in anticipation of living in a greater reality of the love of God for me.

In Jesus' Name I pray,
Amen.

Scripture References

Give thanks to the God of gods, for his steadfast love endures forever. Give thanks to the Lord of lords: His love endures forever. To him who alone does great wonders, His love endures forever. Psalm 136:2-3

"...Fear not, for I have redeemed you; I have called you by your name; You are Mine." Isaiah 43:1

But God demonstrates his own love for us in this: While we were still sinners, Christ died for us. Since we have now been justified by his blood, how much more shall we be saved from God's wrath through him! Romans 5:8-9

"Yet in all these things we are more than conquerors through Him who loved us. For I am persuaded that neither death nor life, nor angels nor principalities nor powers, nor things present nor things to come, nor height nor depth, nor any other created thing, shall be able to separate us from the love of God which is in Christ Jesus our Lord." Romans 8:37-39

And so we know and rely on the love God has for us. God is love. Whoever lives in love lives in God, and God in them.
1 John 4:16

TO LOVE LIKE JESUS

When Jesus looked out over the crowds of people who were following Him only for what they could get from Him, He did not hold their lack of pure motives against them. He was moved by compassion for them. He longed for them to know His Father. He fed them. He healed them. He gave them the truth, offered them the Kingdom. Without expecting anything in return. He loved them. Unconditionally. He calls us to love in this same way. And His Holy Spirit equips us to do just that.

Prayer

Heavenly Father,
It is my desire to glorify Your Name in all I say and do. Most, especially in how I treat my husband and our children. I thank You for Your great love for me. Being rooted and grounded in Your love, show me how to allow You to demonstrate Your love for others through me, especially those in my household. In this way, others will know I am Your disciple. I realize that doing so means often I will have to love even when the actions and words of others hurt me. In those times, when I am hurt, help me to remember that You exemplified the greatest love for me by dying for my sins when I was your enemy. I choose to do love (be patient, kind, humble, honoring, slow to anger, etc.), despite how I feel. Thank You, Holy Spirit, I do not have to rely on myself to love like Jesus. You are the one who pours God's love into my heart and enables me to love others as myself.
In Jesus' Name I pray,
Amen

Scripture References

And hope does not put us to shame, because God's love has been poured out into our hearts through the Holy Spirit, who has been given to us. Romans 5:5

Love is patient, love is kind. It does not envy, it does not boast, it is not proud. It does not dishonor others, it is not self-seeking, it is not easily angered, it keeps no record of wrongs. Love does not delight in evil but rejoices with the truth. It always protects, always trusts, always hopes, always perseveres. 1 Corinthians 13:4-7

May the Lord lead your hearts into a full understanding and expression of the love of God and the patient endurance that comes from Christ. 2 Thessalonians 3:5

Dear friends, let us love one another, for love comes from God. Everyone who loves has been born of God and knows God. 1 John 4:7

We love because He first loved us. 1 John 4:19

TO REST IN THE SUFFICIENCY OF CHRIST

I don't know about you, but when I'm waiting for things to change it is easy to become obsessed. When I'm hurt, I focus on relief. When I'm sick, I fixate on getting well. When I lack, I want provision. When the remedy for my situation doesn't happen within a comfortable timeframe, I become preoccupied with finding solutions. During a struggle, I sensed the Lord asking me a question, "Am I alone enough?" Is it enough that I have Him even if I have an illness in which He allows me to struggle? Is it enough that I can call Him Father when He doesn't answer in the way, I hope? Is His love for me enough when others reject me? For us to be able to love others who do not love us yet, or may never reciprocate that love, God alone must become enough.

Prayer

Heavenly Father,
Even in times when I am consistent in prayer, I find I seek You more for relief from suffering, a need, or a desire in my heart than I seek You for You. Although it is good for me to come to You for everything, far too often I seek Your deeds and not Your face. Father, I repent for placing Your promises above Your Person. Please forgive me for not always demonstrating in my life and prayers that You are the prize. According to Psalm 68:19, You load us up with benefits every single day. There is not a concern I have You will not perfect. Your will is not always understandable, but You are always good. Your plans for me are always best. You are always trustworthy. Help me to rest in Your character so that You become more real to me than what I experience in this life. Refocus my heart so that relationship with You becomes my chief pursuit. Thank You for being my salvation, strength, hope, peace, and all that I need. You, alone, are enough.
In Jesus' Name,
Amen.

Scripture References

"The Lord your God in your midst, The Mighty One, will save;
He will rejoice over you with gladness, He will quiet you with
His love, He will rejoice over you with singing." Zephaniah 3:17

"But whoever is united with the Lord is one with Him in spirit"
1 Corinthians 6:17

"Now you are the body of Christ, and each one of you is a part
of it" 1 Corinthians 12:27

"...and in Christ you have been brought to fullness. He is the
head over every power and authority." Colossians 9:10

"But you are a chosen people, a royal priesthood, a holy
nation, God's special possession, that you may declare the
praises of Him who called you out of darkness into His
wonderful light." 1 Peter 2:9

TO GROW IN GRATITUDE

I go through the spurts where I try to eat healthy and exercise consistently. My husband and I went to the fitness center where we had a membership. Like many times before, I jumped on the treadmill and began my workout. I must have lost my mind because at some point I began to dance. On the treadmill. As it was moving. To make a long story short, I tore the MCL in my left knee. Not my best moment. Laid up, I started thinking how blessed I was I tore my MCL when my husband was home instead of travelling. Gratefulness grew in my heart from there and the tear in my knee became less bothersome. Gratitude flows from a heart that has learned to appreciate the moments. If we're not naturally grateful, the Holy Spirit can teach us how to become grateful.

Prayer

Father, there is so much I have for which I'm grateful. There is Your great love and compassion, the salvation I've received through faith in Jesus Christ, my husband, our children, and so much more. But all too often, I focus on what I don't have, what I'm still waiting for, and what I want to change. I repent for allowing my complaints to eclipse your goodness. Forgive me for my self-focused thinking. Holy Spirit, please help me to grow in gratitude, to remember the goodness of the Lord and rest in His faithfulness. Help me to be content in whatever circumstance I may find myself because I have Christ and He strengthens me. I know You are working out Your best on my behalf. I choose to humble myself before You in adoration and gratitude.
In Jesus' Name,
Amen.

Scripture References

That my glory may sing your praise and not be silent. O Lord my God, I will give thanks to you forever! Psalm 30:12

Praise the Lord! Oh give thanks to the Lord, for he is good, for his steadfast love endures forever! Psalm 106:1

Do not be anxious about anything, but in everything by prayer and supplication with thanksgiving let your requests be made known to God. Philippians 4:6

And whatever you do, in word or deed, do everything in the name of the Lord Jesus, giving thanks to God the Father through him. Colossians 3:17

Give thanks in all circumstances; for this is the will of God in Christ Jesus for you. 1 Thessalonians 5:18

TO FORGIVE OFFENSES

I'm sure you have read, or heard, or may have even said, "Unforgiveness is like drinking poison expecting the other person to die." That is more than a metaphor. Unforgiveness hurts the offended exponentially more than the offender. Harboring unforgiveness deafens the Father's ears to our prayers. An inability to allow for the errors of others while asking God for mercy for oneself places a wall between the offended and the Lord. When we are unwilling to forgive those who have hurt us, the Father becomes unwilling to forgive our sins. Unforgiveness gives pride permission to kick God off the thrones of our hearts, replacing God with self. Effectively dealing with unforgiveness will help us wait in a way that glorifies God.

Prayer

Father, I'm sorry for harboring unforgiveness in my heart. The weight of offense is crushing my ability to love freely and keeping me from receiving Your much-needed forgiveness. Set me free from the prison offense has erected around my heart and life. I bring my hurts to You, the Only one who can heal my aching heart. I give up the right to be compensated. I no longer wait for an apology, or for a feeling. I choose to forgive (insert name(s) here) for offending me. I choose to clean their slate and hold no record of wrong against them, in the same way You have forgiven me. Help me develop a thick skin but keep a tender heart so I can remain free from offense. Father, I ask that if I have done anything to offend them please heal them from any damage I may have caused and rescue them from the prison of unforgiveness as well. Give me the strength to humble myself and ask for their forgiveness.

In Jesus' Name,

Amen

Scripture References

He heals the brokenhearted, And binds up their wounds."
Psalm 147:3

For if you forgive others their trespasses, your heavenly Father will also forgive you, but if you do not forgive others their trespasses, neither will your Father forgive your trespasses.
Matthew 6:14-15

Then Peter came up and said to him, "Lord, how often will my brother sin against me, and I forgive him? As many as seven times?" Jesus said to him, "I do not say to you seven times, but seventy times seven. Matthew 18:21-22

Pay attention to yourselves! If your brother sins, rebuke him, and if he repents, forgive him, and if he sins against you seven times in the day, and turns to you seven times, saying, 'I repent,' you must forgive him." Luke 17:3-4

Beloved, never avenge yourselves, but leave it to the wrath of God, for it is written, "Vengeance is mine, I will repay, says the Lord." Romans 12:19

TO GET OVER THE PAST

Stacy desperately needed to speak to her dear friend about "a problem in her marriage." After 45 minutes of venting, Stacy took a long and noisy sip of tea, placed her teacup on the table, then looked at her friend with tears shimmering in her eyes, "Then he told me he wasn't sure he made the best choice marrying me!" The words Stacy's husband spoke to her made the friend's heart hurt and she sympathized with the pain Stacy felt. However, she sympathized more when Stacy told her the story two years ago! Not only had Stacy's husband regretted and apologized for those words, but he followed up that apology with counseling and courting in an effort to reassure Stacy of his love and commitment. Stacy just won't let it go and it's ruining her relationship, not to mention her peace of mind. She will tell you she has forgiven her husband, but she is holding on to the hurt she felt and anchoring her relationship to the past.

Prayer

Father, it was for freedom's sake alone that I have been made free through the blood of Jesus Christ. I refuse to allow regret, shame, sadness, anger, or guilt over the past to hold me in bondage any longer. I also refuse to keep the present hostage to the past mistakes of others. Your servant Paul, a former murderer of Your people, said, "I don't pretend to have it all but this one thing I do. Forgetting those things which are behind me, and reaching for what lies ahead, I press towards the mark for the prize of the high calling of God in Christ Jesus" Lord, enable me by Your power and Spirit to do the same. I agree with Your word and no longer consider the things of old. I thank You for doing a new thing in my heart, my home, my marriage, and my family. For making a way, bringing new life, and creating a refreshing spring in places that were dry. Alleluia!
In Jesus' Name
Amen.

Scripture References

Remember not the former things, nor consider the things of old. Behold, I am doing a new thing; now it springs forth, do you not perceive it? I will make a way in the wilderness and rivers in the desert. Isaiah 43:18-19

There is therefore now no condemnation for those who are in Christ Jesus. Romans 8:1

Therefore, if anyone is in Christ, he is a new creation. The old has passed away; behold, the new has come. 2 Corinthians 5:17

Let all bitterness and wrath and anger and clamor and slander be put away from you, along with all malice. Be kind to one another, tenderhearted, forgiving one another, as God in Christ forgave you. Ephesians 4:31-32

Brothers, I do not consider that I have made it my own. But one thing I do: forgetting what lies behind and straining forward to what lies ahead, I press on toward the goal for the prize of the upward call of God in Christ Jesus. Philippians 3:13-14

TO HAVE A SENSE OF HUMOR

As our then 19-year-old son (my stepson) and I were enjoying a drive one day, I was jaw-jacking for about five minutes straight before I turned to him and noticed he had his earbuds in. I smiled as I tapped him and asked, "Are you listening?" He took a bud out of one ear and replied, "Huh?" To which I responded, "You're listening, but, apparently, not to me." We looked at each other for one beat then fell out laughing. Life is short. Laugh. A lot. Laugh loudest when the joke is at your own expense. A good sense of humor goes a very long way towards creating an environment for stepfamily bonding.

Prayer

Father, Your Kingdom is not meat nor drink but it is righteous, peace and joy in the Holy Spirit. I pray joy would simply explode in our family. Help us to create an atmosphere where laughter and fun is part of our family culture. Develop in each of us a healthy sense of humor which can laugh even at ourselves. Help us to not take everything so seriously but to recognize and capitalize on opportunities for joy and humor. Help us to see where joy is breaking through even the most mundane situations and enjoy our time to laugh.

In Jesus' Name
Amen.

Scripture References

He will yet fill your mouth with laughter, and your lips with shouting. Job 8:21

You have put more joy in my heart than they have when their grain and wine abound. Psalm 4:7

Be glad in the Lord, and rejoice, O righteous, and shout for joy, all you upright in heart! Psalm 32:11

Then our mouth was filled with laughter, and our tongue with shouts of joy; then they said among the nations, "The Lord has done great things for them." Psalm 126:2

Strength and dignity are her clothing, and she laughs at the time to come. Proverbs 31:25

A time to weep, and a time to laugh; a time to mourn, and a time to dance; Ecclesiastes 3:4

FOR MY FAMILY

"I don't know if we're going to make it!" Leslie's tears soaked up ½ a box of tissues before she finished telling us what happened. Married only three years, she and Gary found themselves at, what seemed to them, an unsurpassable stalemate. They were on the brink of divorce. The "yours, mine and ours" dynamic of stepfamily living tore into their fragile union. Then Leslie realized although they had counseled, argued, stonewalled, and ignored, they had yet to pray. As a last-ditch effort, they made a commitment to pray together for their family for at least five minutes every day. Seven years later they celebrated their 10-year anniversary by renewing their vows. It wasn't easy, and several times they nearly threw in the towel, but they remained faithful to pray. Praying for their family softened their hearts and invited the power of God into their circumstances.

Prayer

Father, I acknowledge You as the true head of our family, with the right to direct and use this family for Your glory. I submit my will to Your will in every area of my life. Especially in this family. You have given us everything we need pertaining to life and godliness. You are at work in us giving us the desire and the ability to accomplish Your will. Help us to respect and honor each other. Knit our hearts together. Make us one and teach us to love one another. Father, it gets very hard sometimes, but I refuse to give up. Instead, I hold on to Your promises. We can do all things through Christ who strengthens us. Even succeed as a stepfamily. Thank You. Your grace is accomplishing in and through us what we cannot accomplish on our own. Thank You for moving in our family.

In Jesus' Name,
Amen.

Scripture References

But if serving the Lord seems undesirable to you, then choose
for yourselves this day whom you will serve, whether the gods
your ancestors served beyond the Euphrates, of the gods of
the Amorites, in whose land you are living. But as for me and
my household, we will serve the Lord. Joshua 24:15

God sets the solitary in families; He brings out those who are
bound into prosperity; but the rebellious dwell in a dry land.
Psalm 68:6

Your wife will be like a fruitful vine within your house; your
children will be like olive shoots around your table. Psalm
128:3

He and all his family were devout and God-fearing; he gave
generously to those in need and prayed to God regularly. Acts
10:2

However, each one of you also must love his wife as he loves
himself, and the wife must respect her husband. Ephesians
5:33

Fathers, do not exasperate your children; instead, bring them
up in the training and instruction of the Lord. Ephesians 6:4

TO KNOW I'M NEVER ALONE

As I sat by the river, heartache isolated me from the laughing children and strolling lovers. Life was generous in that riverside park, but I didn't want to be amongst those who were enjoying living. I was tired. Tired of trying. Tired of questioning. Tired of fighting. Tired of thinking. I'd never felt so utterly isolated and defeated. My 17-year marriage was over. I would soon discover the other woman I suspected existed was a reality. It would be an additional four months of a constant barrage of vitriol before we were officially divorced. I had felt God's presence many times throughout the nearly two-year journey but at that moment all I felt was alone. Then a hand reached through the fog of despair and clasped mine. I turned to the friend God had sent to sit in the terrible aloneness with me. A faith fire lit in my heart as this one truth overcame the lies: I have never been nor will I ever be alone.

Prayer

Father, sometimes I feel so alone in this stepmom journey. There are moments it seems as if there is no one I can talk to who will understand the dynamics I live in or the emotions I wrestle with. However, I know this is a lie straight from the enemy of my soul. I refuse to agree with his lie no matter how I feel. Your steadfast love never ceases, and Your mercies never come to an end. They are new every morning and I am never left in need of anything, even companionship. Your Word says I do not serve a high priest who has not been touched by the feelings of my weaknesses. Your word tells me Your presence is with me in whatever situation I face, to lead, guide, encourage, and strengthen me to endure. Thank You for understanding how I feel even though I may be embarrassed to say it to You. Thank You for being the Rock I can run to and lean on. Thank You for sending people at the right time to be a tangible reminder of Your nearness. Help me to stay anchored on the truth that You are with me always.
In Jesus' Name,

Amen

Scripture References

The eternal God is your refuge, And underneath are the everlasting arms; Deuteronomy 33:27

"Whether you turn to the right or to the left, your ears will hear a voice behind you, saying "This is the way; walk in it." Isaiah 30:21

Fear not, for I am with you; Be not dismayed, for I am your God. I will strengthen you, Yes, I will help you, I will uphold you with My righteous right hand." Isaiah 41:10

When you pass through the waters, I will be with you; And through the rivers, they shall not overflow you. When you walk through the fire, you shall not be burned, Nor shall the flame scorch you." Isaiah 43:2

"Let your conduct be without covetousness; be content with such things as you have. For He Himself has said, 'I will never leave you nor forsake you.' So we may boldly say: 'The LORD is my helper; I will not fear. What can man do to me?'"
Hebrews 13:5-6

TO ENDURE IN DOING GOOD

"You are to treat him with compassion." Those words were spoken to me by the holy, just, and completely incomprehensible God I love and trust. These were His instructions to me as I dealt with living in a house with a man who was divorcing me, seeing another woman, and declaring his hatred of me quite frequently through word and deed. A few months after hearing that invitation to become more Christ-like, I laid across my bed and cried out in despair, "Lord, I cannot do this any longer. I give up!" Twenty minutes after that declaration, I received a phone call from a friend who said, "You breezed across my mind and the Lord told me to call you to say, "Don't give up. He is with you." God will strengthen us with His grace to keep going and reward us with good as we obey Him.

Prayer

Father, the thing I want most is to please You and hear the words, "Well done, good and faithful servant!" But the road stretches long before me. Help me to run well the race You have given me. And help me to run it with patience. I want to finish strong. Thank You Lord. When I am weak You give me Your strength. When I am tired You provide times of refreshing. When I am emotionally dried up, out of my belly flows rivers of living water through Your Holy Spirit. Help me to stop pushing so hard and just rest in you so I won't burn out. Help me realize when I need to rest physically and retreat mentally to be refreshed by Your presence. When I'm tempted to give up, keep me mindful of the harvest I will reap in my family if I continue to press forward. I praise You now for strength to endure. In Jesus' Name,
Amen.

Scripture References

"And we know that all things work together for good to those who love God, to those who are the called according to His purpose." Romans 8:28

Love never gives up on people. It never stops trusting, never loses hope, and never quits. 1 Corinthians 13:7

"And He said to me, "My grace is sufficient for you, for My strength is made perfect in weakness." Therefore most gladly I will rather boast in my infirmities, that the power of Christ may rest upon me." 2 Corinthians 12:9

Let us not become weary in doing good, for at the proper time we will reap a harvest if we do not give up. Galatians 6:9

I can do all things through Christ who strengthens me. Philippians 4:13

Keep yourselves in the love of God, waiting for the mercy of our Lord Jesus Christ that leads to eternal life. Jude 1:21

TO FIND NEEDED SUPPORT

I'm going to date myself somewhat, but I really enjoyed the Flintstone re-runs when I was a little girl. Let the record show I did not say, "first-runs." I especially enjoyed episodes in which there was singing. In one episode, Fred and Barney were judging a beauty contest for their lodge. After Wilma and Betty entered the contest Fred and Barney awarded their wives the crown. The pageant song began with the line: "We searched high and low for Ms. Water Buffalo..." It's a line I sing whenever I am searching for a needed item I've misplaced. Stepmoms need specific support which is hard to find. God has a ready supply of support available for you, Stepmom Sister. And He knows how to direct you so that you find exactly what you need.

Prayer

Father, You are the God who is with His children. We are not left to our own devices. We are not left to stumble along in darkness. You have brought me into Your Kingdom of Light and You lead me by Your word. I thank You for ample provision to fulfill the Stepmom assignment You have given me. You place the right resources in my hands at the right time. You bring the right persons across my path to help me in this journey. Because of Your great love You give me the desire and ability to please You as a stepmom. It is Your delight that I succeed as a wife, mother, and stepmother. I get exactly what is needed from the storehouse of Your supply. I ask that you alert my eyes to the support You have already provided for me. Alleluia!
In Jesus' Name,
Amen

Scripture References

My soul, wait silently for God alone, For my expectation is from Him. He only is my rock and my salvation; He is my defense; I shall not be moved. In God is my salvation and my glory; The rock of my strength, And my refuge, is in God. Trust in Him at all times, you people; Pour out your heart before Him; God is a refuge for us. Psalm 62:5-8

"If I say, "My foot slips," Your mercy, O Lord, will hold me up. In the multitude of my anxieties within me, Your comforts delight my soul" Psalm 94:18-19

My help comes from the Lord, Who made heaven and earth. Psalm 121:2

Then Jesus spoke to them again, saying, "I am the light of the world. He who follows Me shall not walk in darkness, but have the light of life. John 8:12

Therefore humble yourselves under the mighty hand of God, that He may exalt you in due time, casting all your care upon Him, for He cares for you. 1 Peter 5:6-7

WISDOM TO LIVE IN STEP

Sometimes I just don't know what to do. And even when I know what to do, I don't always know how to do what I know to do to get the best results. For example, I know to lose weight I must eat right and exercise. Yet, I've been battling my weight for the last 20 years. Clearly, it's not enough to have knowledge. We must know how to apply it. We need strategies. We need clarity. We need direction. We need wisdom. Thank goodness there is an endless source of wisdom in our Heavenly Father.

Prayer

Father, there are times I do not know what to do. Even when I think I know what to do I don't necessarily know how or when to do it. However, You, the all-wise God, the Alpha and Omega who knows the beginning from the end, have invited me to ask You when I need wisdom. Father, I need Your wisdom. You made my children and know exactly what they need from me and what will reach their hearts. Thank You for directing me in how to parent each of them. Give me insight, help me to see them as You do. Show me when I need to step back. Show me when I need to press in. Most of all, be the Lord of my mothering. All too often I've leaned on my own intelligence and limited understanding. I repent and commit my ways to You. I humble myself before You and ask You to lead me in the way I should go.
In Jesus' Name,
Amen.

Scripture References

The steps of a good man are ordered by the Lord, And He delights in his way. Though he fall, he shall not be utterly cast down; For the Lord upholds him with His hand.
Psalm 37:23-24

God is our refuge and strength, A very present help in trouble.
Psalm 46:1

Trust in the LORD with all your heart and lean not on your own understanding; in all your ways acknowledge Him, and He shall direct your paths. Proverbs 3:5-6

For we do not have a High Priest who cannot sympathize with our weaknesses, but was in all points tempted as we are, yet without sin. Let us therefore come boldly to the throne of grace, that we may obtain mercy and find grace to help in time of need. Hebrews 4:15-16

If any of you lacks wisdom, you should ask God, who gives generously to all without finding fault, and it will be given to you. James 1:5

NOTES

Waiting Wail

1. McCallum, Tom. "All Things Come to Those Who Wait." Tom McCallum, 13, January 2019, https://tommccallum.com/2019/01/13/all-things-come-to-those-who-wait/#gsc.tab=0

Chapter 3: Shark Bait

1. Godin, Seth. Taking Umbrage. Facebook, 21 February 2014, https://www.facebook.com/sethgodin/posts/10100809046326730. Accessed 1, Dec. 2019
2. Bevere, John. The Bait of Satan: Living Free from the Deadly Trap of Offense, Lake Mary: Creation House, 1994. Print
3. Bevere. The Bait of Santa: Living Free from the Deadly Trap of Offense

Chapter 9: The (He)Art of Renegotiation

1. Butler, Summer. Blended: Aligning the Hierarchy of Heart and Home, Greenville: Kingdom Winds, 2020. Print
2. Laurie, Greg. "Did You Know That Jesus is Praying for You?" Salem Web Network, 14, November 2019, https://www.biblestudytools.com/bible-study/topical-studies/did-you-know-jesus-is-praying-for-you.html

Chapter 11: Sturdy Love

1.   Shumake, Cheryl. Joyful, Joy-full: The Hidden Treasure of a Surrendered Life, Maitland: Xulon Press, 2015. Print

Chapter 16: Safe Shepherds

1.   Butler. Blended: Aligning the Hierarchy of Heart and Home

Chapter 17: This Heart is on Fire

1.   "To fall in love with God" n.d. Raphael Simon Quote, Thoughts About God, https://thoughts-about-god.com/quotes_/raphael-simon-quote "
2.   Piper, John. Desiring God: Meditations of a Christian Hedonist. Colorado Springs: Multnomah Books; Revised and Expanded Edition, 2003. Print
3.   Evans, Tony. The Power of Knowing God. Eugene: Harvest House Publishers, 2020. Print
4.   Kraby, Clayton. "Fellowship of the Unashamed: A Martyr's Prayer." Reasonable Theology, n.d, https://reasonabletheology.org/fellowship-of-the-unashamed-a-martyrs-prayer/

ACKNOWLEDGEMENTS

I am so grateful for the prayers, support, and handholding which helped get this book out of my heart and onto pages.

To the editors who polished; Rachel Song of Songbird Editing, thank you so much for your work on the first draft. To Ashara Giles-Jones of Ashara Ylana LLC Editing Services, thank you for refining. You are an exceptional partner.

To the brilliant team at The Inspired Studio, LLC: Nicole Peavy, Jamie Bonds, Luverta Reames, and Serena Boyd, and the ladies who, along with them, comprise the Stepmom Sanity team: Mom, Dr. Tahira Smith, and Germaine Simms: I don't even know where to begin. You are the A-team for sure! Thank you for praying, branding, coaching, the cover design, feedback, keeping us on track with God's vision for our ministry, and oh, so much more. You breathe life into the journey.

To the Launch Team, thank you for being the first readers, reviewers, and trumpeters of Waiting to be Wanted. You are appreciated more than you know.

To the Tribe, my God-given sisters, thank you for being my safe place.

To my family; my supportive, loving, hero, Jonathan, my beautiful Peanut, Kayla, my bonus blessings, Chakia, Briana, and Jay; I am so grateful to the Lord for each you. You have filled my life with immeasurable joy.

To April, the mother of my bonus children, thank you...you are a blessing.

Most important, to my Lord and Savior, Jesus Christ, to You be all the glory!

Hope for Stepmoms Who are
There, From Stepmoms Who've
Been There!

@StepmomSanity

www.StepmomSanity.com

Made in the USA
Monee, IL
09 June 2021

70768744R00155